WOUNDED RANGERS

Under enemy fire in Afghanistan

Dominic Hagans

Warrant Officer, 1st Battalion Royal Irish Regiment

WOUNDED
RANGERS

Under enemy fire in Afghanistan

Mereo is an imprint of Memoirs Publishing

Published by Mereo

Mereo is an imprint of Memoirs Publishing

25 Market Place, Cirencester, Gloucestershire GL7 2NX
Tel: 01285 640485, Email: info@mereobooks.com
www.memoirspublishing.com, www.mereobooks.com

Wounded Rangers - Under enemy fire in Afghanistan

ISBN: 978-1-909544-58-1

CONTENTS

*Greater love hath no man than this, that
a man lay down his life for his friends*

(John 15:13)

INTRODUCTION

I was born on a small estate called Castle Vale in Birmingham, which is why I am generally known to my mates as Brummie. I joined the army in June 1990 and went on to take part in several operations around the world.

In June 2008 I was serving in Afghanistan as a Warrant Officer in the 1st Battalion the Royal Irish Regiment. My battalion was part of Operation Herrick 8 (Operation Herrick is the codename under which all British operations in the war in Afghanistan are conducted – Herrick 8 took place from April-October 2008).

More than 400 British personnel have so far been killed in the Afghan conflict and thousands injured, along with many more from other nations. On September 11 2008, I became one of the injured when an improvised bomb (IED) exploded under my vehicle, wrecking my legs and putting an end to my active service.

Not many people understand the devastating nature of the injuries sustained in the Afghan conflict as a result of IEDS and high-velocity bullets. I hope this book will give an insight into what soldiers are going through daily and how it affects so many people at home.

This book is a compilation of true stories from me and my comrades from the front line. All the proceeds will go to the welfare fund of the 1st'Battalion the Royal Irish Regiment, who look after our wounded and need money to help them adapt and adjust to their injuries.

These stories cover the lives of several wounded soldiers, including myself, and the effects of our injuries, as well as other perspectives on the war, including that of a mother whose son was critically injured. The events that led to the injury are described, followed by the story of the soldier who led the casualty evacuation (casevac). Some of these soldiers have made it back to work, but most, including myself, are still battling to get back to some kind of normality.

THE DISTRICTS OF HELMAND PROVINCE

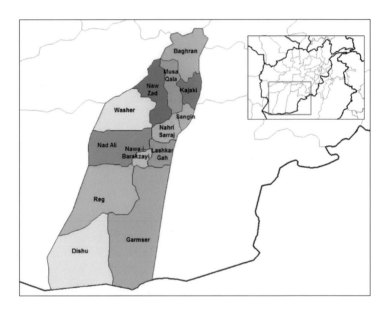

ACKNOWLEDGEMENTS

I would like to thank all the staff at Selly Oak Hospital, Queen Elizabeth's Hospital in Birmingham and Kings College Hospital in London. I also would like to thank all the welfare staff at the 1st Battalion The Royal Irish Regiment for all their time and dedication throughout my recovery, especially to Capt Nigel Bradley QGM for looking after my family during my incident, and to Capt John Millar for looking after my recovery.

Without the extremely professional attitude of staff at Headley Court, the Defence Medical Rehabilitation Centre near Epsom, many more soldiers would be lost. Thank you all at Headley Court for helping with so many wounded men and women.

I would sincerely like to thank my wife Stacy, my children Sian and Quinn, my mother and father, Doris and Dominic, and my brothers and sister. I know I have put you all through hell over the last three years.

I would like to say 'thank you' to C/Sgt Gilchrist for his part in Op Herrick 4, and Capt Whitmarsh for his part in Op Herrick 13.

Finally, I want to thank Mrs Josie McKinney for her story about her son Alistair. I know it was hard for her because it brought back so many bad memories.

CHAPTER 1

MY PERSONAL 9/11

DOMINIC HAGANS

My battalion, 1 Royal Irish, was deployed as the OMLT (Operational Mentoring and Liaison Team) responsible for training the Afghan National Army (ANA). Whilst operating in Marjah during July 2008 OMLT 4 had survived several contacts with the Taliban and I had been shot in the boot, lost my vehicle door to an RPG attack (see chapter 6) and encountered several ambushes. After getting away with it so many times I thought the luck of the Irish was with us, though we had lost an outstanding soldier in battle in Marjah. I thought to myself that we couldn't get any more thrown at us - we had had it all. But I was wrong.

In August we headed south to the notorious Garmsir area. We were to take over from our American friends there, and the handover went very well. We patrolled daily with the Yanks until we were happy with the Tactical Area of Responsibility. After we had taken control and the Yanks had left, my OC (Officer

Commanding), Major Rob Armstrong, and I had decided that our men did not have enough overhead protection and needed engineer support.

On the September 11 2008 (yes, 9/11) I took a two-vehicle patrol to visit my men and to enable a captain from the engineers to carry out his recce. We had been to Stella and Alma and all was well. At about 1215 hrs we headed south towards Patrol Base 1. We were about 1.5 kilometres south of Alma when suddenly, from nowhere, I was engulfed in one hell of an explosion.

I felt an initial surge of pain in my legs then, just the way they make it look in the war movies, time stood still. I felt I was moving very slowly and floating in the air. It seemed as if I was there for ages. Finally I was lying on the ground.

I sat up and looked to my right. I could see the radio, which had landed by me. I picked it up and found it was still working. I sent an initial contact report, receiving no answer, although I later found out that they had heard me.

I looked down, and what happened next seemed to take place in slow motion. I could see that my left leg was hanging off below the knee. My right leg was shattered. I couldn't even administer morphine, because my body armour and helmet had been blown off by the blast and the morphine was in my armour. It was mad, because I should have been in terrible pain, but somehow I wasn't.

I looked up to see Cpl Alan Boyle and Sig Lee

Townsend moving towards us. I shouted at them to bring the metal detectors. As they were coming over, I needed to know my crew were OK, so I shouted at Capt Ben Power. He shouted back, and I was very relieved to hear his voice.

Then I shouted for Cpl Cecil Carter. There was no response. Please God no, I was thinking, but then I heard his voice too. I was overwhelmed with relief to know he was alive.

Cpl Boyle arrived with the men and they put me on a stretcher. It was a funny feeling being put on the stretcher separately from my left leg, which was only just attached. The team then took us back to Alma, where they gave us first aid. Blood was flowing out of my leg and I felt my heart racing. I was struggling for air, and must have been in shock. I felt my eyes starting to close and asked Cpl Dave Imrie to tell my kids I loved them. My eyes closed and I thought I was gone, but then I felt a smack around the face and a scream of 'Brummie!'

I opened my eyes. As soon as I did so I felt a sudden pain in my left leg - it was the tourniquet being tightened.

I could see an Apache helicopter in the sky, so I knew help was at hand. The Chinook couldn't land where we were, so I had to be moved 100 metres by stretcher to a new landing point.

Once I was safely on board I felt I would be in good hands, but I no longer knew what was really going on. That must have been the morphine.

I remember being in the hospital at Camp Bastion, the main military base, with floods of light everywhere. Sometime later I awoke to the thankful faces of the CO and the RSM, and it was good to see them. I was in pain, but still alive. I could see that my leg was a mess but it was still there, thank God.

I know I had several visitors that day, but I couldn't have told you who came as I was so out of it on morphine.

The following day, September 12, I was flown back to the UK, destined for Selly Oak Hospital in Birmingham. The flight took 11 hours in total. Over the first 48 hours after I arrived at Selly Oak I went through several operations to repair my legs. The doctors did an outstanding job. They had to rebuild my lower left leg, with muscles and tissue transfers from both thighs. I had bolts and plates put in where the blast had taken my bones apart. My left foot and ankle were shattered and had to be rebuilt and fixed together with a cage. My right leg was broken in two places and the talus (heel bone) in my right ankle was broken.

I spent nearly seven weeks in Selly Oak Hospital. The staff was brilliant; if it hadn't been for them I would never have made such a fast recovery. On October 27 I was moved to Headley Court, the Defence Medical Rehabilitation Centre in Surrey, to begin my rehabilitation. I knew it was going to be a long-drawn-out process, but I will never give up.

Having lived to tell the tale, I would like to say the

casevac chain – the evacuation system for wounded personnel - does work, and is very effective, and the welfare I have received by all is second to none.

I would like to say thank you to Captain Bradley and his team and to John and Elaine, two of the civilian personnel drafted in to help the battalion with welfare cases like mine - thank you for your time and effort. Finally I would like to thank all the doctors and nurses who have helped me to get through this.

My injuries? Well, all you need to know is that Brummie is alive and well.

CHAPTER 2

RESCUE AND EVACUATION

C/SGT BRETT CUNNINGHAM-EDDAS

I was deployed late on to Operation Herrick 8 after returning to 1 Royal Irish from a posting to our sister battalion, 2 Royal Irish. I knew 1 Royal Irish had been deployed as the OMLT (Operational Mentoring and Liaison Team) responsible for training the Afghan National Army (ANA).

I arrived in Camp Shorobak, the rear operations base for the Battle Group, with a feeling of trepidation. I knew that arriving late would put me at a disadvantage, as all the teams were already well established and had been operating together for some time. I would therefore have to fit in where I was told.

When I was initially posted into OMLT 4, my first question was to ask who was in charge. The answer quickly came back that it was Major Armstrong (someone I didn't know) and WO2 Dominic Hagans, better known as Brummie, so thank God at least I know somebody. The OMLT and the KANDAK (ANA

Battalion) had just returned from an intensive period of ops and were in the process of training and sorting themselves out ready to push down south into Garmasir.

I was placed into a small six-man team as the 2IC (second in command) commanded by Capt Ray Dalzell. It took a number of days and pit stops into different camps, but eventually we arrived at what would be our new home for the next 2-3 months, PB (Patrol Base) Stella. The OMLT and the ANA KANDAK had all been pushed out on to the eastern flank of Garmasir and taken up a line of PBs and FOBs (Forward Operation Bases) along the eastern side of the main transit route into the DC (District Centre). We

Dominic on the left next to the actor Ross Kemp, three weeks before he was injured.

had taken over from elements of the USMC (United States Marine Corps) and 5 Scots.

PBs Stella, Alma and PB 1 were quickly established and normal routine followed. The OMLT and ANA set about normal security patrols, conducting route clearances and providing security at the PVCPs (permanent vehicle checkpoints) along the main route.

Brummie was based in the DC (the main camp for Garmasir) and had many responsibilities. One of these was to visit all the PBs on a regular basis to ensure both the ANA and the British troops within all locations were doing everything correctly. These visits provided one of the few opportunities for us to meet face to face. It was on one of these visits that the incident happened.

September 11 started like any other, except that I knew Brummie would be visiting with the new OMLT 2IC, Capt Power. He had been posted into the OMLT recently from the PWRR (Princess of Wales' Royal Regiment) which had just taken control of the DC as the Theatre Reserve Battalion. As always, prior to the visit I was busy running around trying to get the ANA to do as they should , ensuring the OMLT guys were sorted and that the PB itself was fit for a visit.

I remember hearing Brummie on the radio stating that he was leaving the DC en route to PB Stella. I knew that the transit time would only be about 15–20 minutes, so I had to get into another gear sorting the place out (my hair was probably on fire at this time). It wasn't long before Brummie, Capt Powers, Bro (Cpl

Boyle) and a medic and a number of others whose names escape me, for which I apologies, arrived in a WMIK (a Land Rover carrying a Weapons Mounted Installation Kit) and PINZ, a military vehicle built with limited armour, used to transport soldiers and small equipment. The kettle (a pot of water over the hexi blocks) was on, always best practice when receiving visitors, especially Brummie, who I knew was partial to a brew.

We all quickly settled down chatting and conducted the normal meet and greet rituals before Capt Dalzell and I briefed the new 2IC. All in all the visit happened quickly and it wasn't long before the visitors mounted up and headed for PB Alma some 800 meters south and visible to the eye from PB Stella.

Following Brummie's departure, my team settled back into normal routine and I specifically remember returning to radio stag (radio sentry). Brummie soon reported that he and his party had arrived and PB Alma and would be going firm for a short period. I acknowledged and relayed this to the DC.

The next thing I remember is Brummie reporting that he was leaving PB Alma for PB 1, which everyone acknowledged. It's what happened next that is fixed in my mind and will be forever. It must have been no more than 30–60 seconds after Brummie's last radio message when I and everyone in my PB heard a large explosion. We all instantly knew, because of the recent radio message and gut instinct, that something had happened to Brummie's convoy.

I remember shouting to the guys outside the radio room 'Brummie's been hit!' and for a few seconds everything happened in slow motion. I ran to the compound wall to look south and saw a large plume of smoke just south of PB Alma. Things then started to happen rapidly. Without being asked, members of my team (Cpl Dave Imrie, LCpl Neil Norton, Rgr (Ranger) Andy Muldrew and Smudger the medic) all started to mount up in the vehicles to go and assist.

It had still only been a few seconds since the explosion and I remember hearing Brummie's voice over the radio: 'Contact IED 'wait out''. My initial thoughts on hearing this was, 'Thank God, they must be OK'. How wrong I was.

Dominic Hagans' vehicle after the IED strike. Notice the ammunition recovered that never went off (rear left wheel)

We got loaded and set off at top speed to PB Alma. We pulled into the courtyard and started to prepare to receive casualties from the convoy. Some of the OMLT and ANA at PB Alma had gone forward to help with the recovery. The PINZ with Bro, properly known as Cpl Alan Boyle, was the first vehicle back, pulling into the courtyard where the boys sprung into action. Everything was manic at this stage, but there are certain things that truly stick in my mind. I have listed the main points below:

- I remember Brummie being pulled out of the back of the PINZ on a stretcher and thinking 'How can he be a casualty? He was the one on the radio!'

- I remember Capt Powers being injured as well – it turned out to be a shattered right leg.

- I remember Smudger (a TA medic) doing an outstanding job organising everyone, sorting out all the MISTs (updates on the casualty's condition to the MERT team en route to casualties) and passing info for the 9 Liner (an initial report sent over the radio with information on type of injury, name of soldier wounded, location of casualties etc). His performance ended up becoming a massive confidence booster for everyone in my team. It later turned out that he was an Arctic exploration medic and more highly qualified than some civilian paramedics.

- I remember Brummie being covered in oil and diesel. All his clothing and equipment were drenched.

■ I remember assisting in the treatment of Brummie's injuries. The thing that sticks in my mind was that his left leg felt like jelly. It was as if there was nothing rigid inside it.

Everyone had their own tasks, and Davy Imrie's was to chat to Brummie and keep him conscious. I remember I went to speak to Brummie a few times, and he kept saying 'Tell Stacy and the kids I love them', to which I replied 'Shut up you nutter, you can tell them yourself when you get to hospital'. However I still remember the sickness in the pit of my stomach every time he said it.

It wasn't long before we heard reports that the MERT (Medical Emergency Response Team) was in the air and en route. We quickly set about sorting out the HLS (helicopter landing site) inside the compound and gathered the smoke grenades to signal it in. The finishing touches were being done to the three casualties (Brummie's top gunner had sustained a broken thumb) in preparation for loading on to the Chinook.

The MERT quickly arrived and proceeded to fly around the PB preparing to land. They attempted to land inside the compound twice, but the dust was too bad and the Chinook caused brownout (invisibility from dust) on both occasions, which forced the pilot to choose a separate one which was used for the extraction. I remember the helicopter lifting and heading off and thinking 'where the fuck does he think he's goin?' I didn't fully understand that the pilot was changing his approach and picking an HLS outside the compound.

The pilot then proceeded to land, and once on the ground we rushed the casualties on stretchers to the new HLS.

Once the casualties were loaded it was over as quickly as it had started. I remember going round all the troops involved to ensure they were OK. Some required a short period of time by themselves to take stock of everything. I later became aware that the incident had impacted on everyone.

Cpl Davy Imrie had done an outstanding and difficult job. While Brummie had been slipping in and out of consciousness he had been saying things like 'I'm dying', 'Oh well that's me' and again 'Tell Stacy and the kids I love them'. Dave had heard all these emotionally-charged comments and continued to reassure him. I felt physically sick when I heard Brummie say these things. I don't think I could have taken many more such comments and not been affected, but Dave listened and responded to them continually. Everyone in the OMLT liked and respected Brummie and this surely only added to the feelings of foreboding.

It was then back to normal routine, because, cruel as it sounds, life does go on. I have been involved with other incidents since Brummie was hurt and each time it has been just as difficult to go on. Something in your mind tells you that you shouldn't carry on as normal - how could you after what has just happened? However that incident and others since have taught me that there is nothing better for soldiers than 'cracking on' and getting straight back into it. There is a difference here between the Armed Forces and any other service that responds to incidents. In the Army 'cracking on' means to put yourself and others into potentially dangerous situations that could easily end like the one just dealt with or worse.

It was a long time before I saw Brummie again, thanks to the rest of the tour and all his rehabilitation procedures. Before I left theatre I did manage to see the wrecked WMIK. I stood there taking in the mangled wreckage, trying to imagine what it must have been like. Let's put it into context, the WMIK is not renowned for its protective capabilities. Everyone in the vehicle is open to the elements, though it does have blast plates and I'm sure they did do something to help during the incident. Those who did the clean-up afterwards reported that the engine was found 20–30 meters from the seat of the explosion. Brummie was sitting inches from the engine, as he was driving. The engine compartment was completely missing; the drivers 'and commanders' seats were totally mangled. I couldn't comprehend what it must have been like to be caught in that explosion, let alone live with the images that would still haunt me to this day had I been involved.

I remember weighing two images up in my head while staring at the damaged vehicle. One was the vehicle itself, and the other was Brummie on the stretcher, injured but alive. The two images didn't compute. I couldn't understand how he was still living and breathing, let alone how he was able to be the first on the radio sending the contact report. Imagine, first being caught in the blast of an IED strong enough to blow the engine 20–30 meters away, then being blown from your vehicle with your leg smashed to pieces, covered in oil and diesel, and still having the frame of mind to command the initial situation. His actions ensured that supporting troops could move rapidly to assist; I think everyone would agree Brummie was utterly professional.

I always respected Brummie, but I respect him even more now. It's not only for his actions on the day and how he conducted himself as a commander during the tour, but how he has conducted himself since his return from tour.

MERT coming to get Dominic for extraction to Camp Bastion.

I cannot even begin to contemplate what the last few years have been like for Brummie, with the number of times he's been in and out of hospital, operations and trips to Headley Court. He has been on crutches, using a walking stick on crutches, and currently he has to endure a large cage device on his leg. It must be difficult, but he has remained loyal to the battalion and in particular the WOs and Sergeants' Mess. He lives and breathes the military and you can tell it pains him not to be able to do the things other soldiers are now doing.

He continually comes back to participate in battalion life where ever possible. He has been a friend and helping hand to other injured soldiers within the battalion, has organized events to raise money for Help for Heroes, and all this while coping with his own injuries and personal life.

I broke my leg prior to Op TELIC 1 and was a complete pain to my family during my convalescence, which only took a few short months. I don't believe I possess the inner strength that Brummie displays each time I see him. It seems that each time there has been another obstacle placed in his path and he always manages to overcome them. These are the reasons he gains everyone's respect.

CHAPTER 3

THE DEFENCE OF MUSA QALA - OPERATION HERRICK 4

C/SGT STEPHEN GILCHRIST

During the initial deployment of OP Herrick, Ranger Platoon was sent in with a 3 Para battle group. It was clear that the battle group was small and needed to be bolstered to help troops on the ground, so a trawl was sent out throughout the companies within the battalion to find people willing to put their names forward to form the further two platoons required to bolster those numbers. The platoons were to be named Barossa and Somme after major Royal Irish victories on the Battlefield, which the platoons hoped to live up to.

It did not take long for those numbers to be found within the battalion, with the men from A and B Company making up Barossa and those from C and D Company making up Somme. The numbers were bolstered further by adding a mortar section to each Platoon to give a heavy punch behind the firepower.

Towards the end of June 2006 the platoons came

together for the first time and conducted a short OPTAG package before flying out to Camp Bastion. This is an Operational Training Advisory Group, a training package put together to update the skills needed to perform a job on the ground, run by highly trained and dedicated soldiers. Before flying out, most of the men had the feeling that this would just be another deployment like Kosovo or Iraq, from which the battalion had just returned at the beginning of the year. However on arriving in Afghanistan it hit home very early that this would turn out to be a completely different operational theatre from any the battalion had seen in many years. The stories from the front line were being passed on from Ranger Platoon, which was based at Camp Bastion as the ARF (Airborne Reaction Force) but had seen heavy fighting in Gersehk.

After a short bedding-in period of seven days, Somme Platoon and the mortar sections were made ready to relieve the Pathfinder Platoon in Musa Qala, which had been under sustained attack as they worked alongside the Danes to help keep the District Centre within the village under ISAF control. A battle group operation was needed to insert Somme Platoon into Musa Qala and help extract the Pathfinders. It came at a price, as a member of the RLC (Royal Logistic Corps) was killed as the battle group extracted back towards the western bank of Musa Qala wadi. The reality of the situation really came to the fore when Cpl Alistair McKinney (Royal Irish) was critically injured as his section took over duties of the Outpost, one of the key Sangers (fortifications) within the District Centre. The injury was felt not only within the platoon in which Ally served but throughout the Royal Irish, as he was a very popular and experienced member of the battalion. The full story is in the next chapter.

Somme Platoon fought alongside the Danes for a period of two weeks in heavy and sustained conflict, during which they formed a close relationship. However at a higher level an agreement was made to move the Danes. Barossa Platoon (Royal Irish) and Company Headquarters which was formed from members of 3 Para would then move in. Again a battle group operation was put in place to extract the Danes from Musa Qala. However Barossa Platoon would fly into a hot landing zone 24 hours before the Danes were to be pulled out of the village. Some members of Somme Platoon were concerned, as the Danes would take all the .50 cals which provided most of the firepower in the District Centre and they would be replaced by GPMGs (general purpose machine guns), which although an extremely good weapon system lacked the reach and punch of the .50 cal.

Barossa Platoon flew into the District Centre before morning prayers, which seemed to catch the Taliban out as what was thought to be a hot landing zone turned out to be relatively peaceful. The extraction of the Danes the next day again went relatively peacefully with no major incidents. However the peace was not to last, as the Taliban probed the District Centre to try and find out the strengths and dispositions of the men and equipment that had been left behind. These attacks intensified over the first few days of Barossa Platoon arriving within the District Centre.

The Taliban were thought to be working in two separate independent groups, but intercepted ICOM messages made by Company Headquarters indicated that a large-scale early morning attack was planned, which would incorporate both sets of groups attacking all four sides of the District Centre. The Taliban did not disappoint, as a heavy weight of firepower was put down on to every Sanger, with the unfortunate death of another British soldier as he helped to man the roof of the JOC.

Although the Taliban set patterns as to when they would attack the District Centre, they did try and mix up how they would carry out the attack.

For a few days they would approach through a series of rat runs and engage the Sangers with small arms, usually initiating the contact with an RPG (rocket-propelled grenade). After that they would then move on to mortaring the compound from a distance. Spotters could be seen on the tops of buildings adjusting their fire on to the compound. It did not take the Taliban long to find the range and this resulted in the unfortunate death of Ranger A Draiva who was killed on the rooftop of the Alamo trying to find cover from the rounds landing inside the compound. Injured alongside Rgr

Draiva was L/Cpl 'Moonbeam' Muirhead. We eventually found out that Moonbeam sadly later died of his battle wounds on the 6th Sept. This again had a major effect on the company, as both these men were held in high esteem by everyone.

One of our main weapons against the Taliban's mortars was our own mortar section, and in Sgt John and Cpl Danny Groves we possessed some of the British Army's most gifted mortar MFCs (mortar fire controllers). The Taliban paid a heavy price, thanks to these two very professional men.

Thankfully these were to be the last fatalities within the company, but sadly not within the Royal Irish. News filtered through from Sangin at the beginning of September that L/Cpl McCulloch had been killed by a mortar round landing close to where he was taking cover. McCulloch was a man everyone in the battalion knew about. He was a character and a practical joker, with many being on the receiving end of his pranks.

These were not the only casualties in the Royal Irish. A mortar strike, again onto Alamo, resulted in eight casualties. One of those was Lt Martin, who needed to have his lungs drained after bits of shrapnel hit him. These men were replaced from a section from 3 Para and came in a short while after the casualties were airlifted out of the district centre.

At the beginning of September 2006 an uneasy truce was called as the village elders wished to return to their homes. They approached the Taliban about calling a ceasefire to allow this to happen. They decided that they had no need for ISAF troops within the village, as part of the deal for them to return was that an exclusion zone was put in place, meaning that the Taliban were not allowed to enter within 2 kms of the village centre.

A deal was put together by the British Hierarchy. The village elders were able to assist in our extraction from the compound through brokering a peace deal with the Taliban. As this was ongoing, large numbers of people started to return to the village, and it felt more like any normal village again instead of the ghost town we had become accustomed to over the previous two months.

It was decided in the end that we would be escorted out of the village by the elders who had brokered the peace. We were to be taken out in local 'Jingly' trucks with the elders leading us to a designated area within the desert to the west of Musa Qala.

There were strong mixed feelings within the Company about our extraction from the village. On top was the obvious sense of relief and excitement about getting back to Bastion and then home, but against that we could not help wondering if three brave men had really had to be killed to achieve what we had just done. This thought was compounded later the next year when the truce between the Taliban and the local elders broke down and once again the village fell into the hands of the Taliban.

CHAPTER 4

CPL ALLY MCKINNEY'S EXTRACTION

SGT P J BRANGAN

August 4 2006 was another blazing hot day in sunny old Afghanistan. My platoon was on sentry duty in Camp Bastion. I had just come back from feeding all our men in the Sangers with Sgt Gilchrist, known to all as Gilly. As I returned, I bumped into Capt. Johnson, the Commander of Somme Platoon. He had just returned from the JOC (Joint Operation Centre) based in Camp Bastion. He gave me and Gilly the good news that we were moving north to a platoon house in Musa Qala, Helmand Province.

I was told we would be moving very shortly to the house, and with the platoon still manning the Sangers in Camp Bastion, lots of work had to be done before we could do so. Gilly and I sat down and conducted a wish list of all the stores, food and ammunition that would be needed to sustain our trip into the unknown. While we were at the tent doing our list, with me holding a brew in one hand and (as usual) a fag in the other, the door of the tent opened and a familiar face walked in. It was Corporal Danny Groves, a fantastic MFC from our battalion, who was being sent with us to the platoon house. He was fantastic at his job and during our stay would become a valuable member of the platoon. We took the Taliban to hell and back several times by bringing awesome firepower down on them.

At 0900 hrs the next day, August 5, the lads had all just finished coming of duty from the Sangers when we sat them down in the conference tent and broke the news to them. Their faces all lit up - at last we were going to do something to take us away from sentry duties in Camp Bastion.

By August 8 we were all packed up and waiting to move. It had become a battle group operation, with 3 Para giving us all the support we needed to move in. Wave after wave of fighting troops from 3 Para had moved into place to provide fire support for us and for the Pathfinder Platoon to move out. It took a few hours for all call signs to secure their areas of responsibilities. We had landed not far from our new home, where we met up with members of the 3 Para battle group. The route up was secure and they were our escort in to the Platoon house and to help extract the Pathfinders from the house.

As we were getting ready to move, we met up with members of Ranger Platoon. As usual Cpl Ally McKinney was giving them the normal slagging banter he was known for. We said our hellos and moved forward to the platoon house.

It was towards evening when we finally arrived at the platoon house, to be met by some of the Danish soldiers who would be living with us for the next three to four weeks. We couldn't believe the amount of Danish vehicles and equipment they had there. It was good to see that they had several .50 Cal machine guns, which would become a lifesaver over the next few weeks, by bringing heavy destruction on the enemy.

The movement in went very peacefully and the handover from the Pathfinders was fairly swift. When nightfall was on us, the Danish platoon sergeant approached me and said 'PJ, your guys will need to start putting their body armour on now and start to get ready for a contact'. The Danes had worked out the timings when the Taliban would attack, and within 20 minutes or so a major contact began.

It was deafening. Several rocket-propelled grenades (RPGs) were fired at the platoon house, followed by a flurry of bullets whizzing over us. The .50 cals on the rooftops were firing at a rapid rate and pushing the Taliban back, thank God for them.

The contact lasted around an hour, with several hundred rounds being fired. There were no casualties on our side, but there must have been some for the enemy, judging by what we had fired at them.

As the contact thinned out we began to stand the blokes down, so they could get on with admin and start settling in to their new home. We started to get a brief from the Danes on what had been happening over the last couple of weeks. They gave us a good rundown, and we were fully in the picture. Over the next few weeks we were to build a fantastic relationship with the Danish guys.

We had now been fully briefed, and I was having a brew and something to eat with the boss, Capt Johnson, when we were informed that we were to take over an outpost the next morning. We chatted and decided that the best section to take over would be Ally McKinney's, as he had the most experience. We got Ally in and briefed him on the next day's activities, and like us he couldn't wait to get stuck in. I told him to go and brief his men, pack kit and go and get some shuteye. I told him I would wake him up at 0600 hrs, in good time for him to get his men ready to take over at 0900. The boss and I went and got our fat heads down for the night.

At 0600 hrs the next day, August 9, I awoke Cpl Alistair McKinney's section so that they could get ready to take over the outpost, which had a fearsome reputation. At 0745 Ally, the boss and I were all having a brew and a chinwag about what we would change about this place and what the lads should expect. During the conversation Ally commented: 'I bet as soon as my fat arse hits the sandbags up there them Taliban bastards will engage us'. That statement will stay with me for the rest of my life.

At 0830 hrs the lads and I had escorted Ally's section to the outpost, where we left Ally to take over and we moved back.

At 0915, as we were doing some administration back at the platoon house, we heard the crack and thump of a round echo over us. Then we heard over the radio being manned by the Danish platoon sergeant contact at the outpost that there had been a casualty. I grabbed my rifle and donned my body armour and helmet. When we got to the outpost there were two Danish medics in front of me. The contact at this point was continuing and Ally's section was holding the Taliban back. The .50 cals started to engage and the noise was deafening. I couldn't hear the medic speaking to me, but he seemed to be saying that we had two casualties.

As we climbed up the ladders to get to the roof, we were coming under fire. In front I saw a lad called Ricky, one of Ally's lads, holding his ear with blood coming out between his hands. The medic grabbed hold of him and had a look. He placed an FFD (first field dressing) on his ear and said it was only a scratch. He directed a soldier to take him to the medical centre.

I moved over to my left and saw Ally on the floor with the medics working like mad on him. It seemed he had a head injury. I crawled over and grabbed his hand, but I was unable to help my friend. The medic was doing the work and I just held his hand. The medic was asking me the man's name, and I told him it was Ally.

At this stage I started to talk to Ally. I told him 'You fucking rat, you are not going to die in this shithole!' He made no response.

We got him down the ladder and on to a stretcher and

then moved him to the medical centre. The fire fight was still going on. The boys were giving the Taliban the good news, inflicting casualties on them and keeping them at bay, but my mind was on Ally in the medical centre.

The doctor continued to work like crazy on Ally, and I have always said it was because of this man's knowledge and valiant efforts that he is alive today. The information had been passed back by the doctor on the radio on Ally's condition and the MERT team was en route, being escorted as normal by an Apache helicopter. It seemed like hours had gone by and the doctor was still working on Ally. The Chinook helicopter had been able to land with cover from the Apache and with the guys still keeping the Taliban's head down, we moved Ally on to the helicopter, which then took him back to Camp Bastion for him to receive lifesaving surgery.

As Ally left, the contact with the enemy started to thin out. We had two casualties plus Ally, and I didn't know if he would make it back to Bastion, let alone live. I stood the men down, then closed them in, briefed them on what happened and told them that Ally was in good hands, knowing myself that he was in a bad way.

In the evening we got the news that he was still alive, thank God. I briefed the blokes, and it seemed to cheer them up that Ally was alive and fighting still. We all knew he was a fighter and if anybody could pull through this, he was the man.

As the tour continued we had several engagements with the enemy and more casualties on the way. When the tour finished and we had moved back to the UK, back up in Inverness I organised a trip for the entire Platoon to go and visit Ally down in Birmingham at the Selly Oak hospital. Some of the blokes knew of his condition and didn't want to see him like that, but we all agreed that we all would do it. I'm glad we did. When we got there we were all upset, but there lay my friend Ally alive and blinking at us all. He even seemed to smile. At this stage some of the guys filled up with tears. I was upset too, but glad to see my fat arse of a friend.

Over the last four years I have seen Ally get better and had several conversations with him. My mate may be in a bad way, but he can still put the one-liners and wisecracks together.

As long I live I will never forget the day I helped to carry my friend off that roof, thinking he was going to die there.

CHAPTER 5

A MOTHER'S STORY

JOSIE MCKINNEY

August 9 2006 was just another ordinary day in the McKinney household. My husband Frank was in the sitting room painting and I was in the kitchen cooking lunch for a team of builders who were up on scaffolding doing some work on our home. The sun was shining and I had left the door open to let some fresh air in.

As I moved to the cooker I heard a voice behind me and turned to see a man with a red clipboard in his hand. He asked if I was Mrs McKinney. I took in his appearance; he was wearing what appeared to be a regimental tie and a dark blue blazer. I replied that I was Mrs McKinney, and he asked if Mr McKinney was at home.

I wondered who he was. I thought that as Frank had recently joined a regimental association he might have come to speak to him about it. I carried on getting plates and cutlery out of the cupboards when he repeated his question, but this time he added the words that no mother ever wants to hear: 'Are you Mrs McKinney, mother of Corporal Alistair McKinney?'

Instantly I knew why he was there. I remember putting my hands over my face and the tears just poured down. So many things went through my mind at the same time.

As I took my hand from my face, I asked him if my son was dead. He replied very solemnly 'No, he is not dead'.

At that moment Frank came into the kitchen with a confused look on his face, looking from me to the military man.

'It's Ally' I said. Poor Frank, like me his eyes filled with tears. I told him he wasn't dead, but I hadn't even asked yet how badly injured he was.

Frank went off at a tangent and started saying things like 'they ask too much from our lads' and telling the poor wee man about how Ally only came out of Iraq in January and had done another course between then and when he was deployed to Afghanistan.

Our visitor asked Frank to take me into the sitting room, where he told us what he knew. He said Ally had been shot at a quarter past five that morning. He had been airlifted to Camp Bastion and was being taken to another country to receive treatment for his injury.

I must have been in shock, because I don't remember him telling us that Ally had been shot through the head, though apparently he did. My mind was in turmoil. How were we going to tell our other kids, Kevin and

Louise? Kevin and Ally had fallen out over a stupid argument the year before, but I was terrified about how my daughter was going to take the news, as Louise and Ally had always been very close. I knew she would go to pieces when she was told.

Frank went to fetch Louise from work and Stan, one of our builders, went with him to drive her car back, as she would be in no fit state to drive when she found out why her dad had come to see her. When she looked up and saw her dad outside the barber's shop she did exactly as I expected - she burst into tears. At first she thought something terrible had happened to me. As her dad cradled her he whispered that it was Ally who had been hurt, and like me she asked if he had been killed.

I phoned my younger son Kevin and all I managed to say was, 'come home, it's Ally'. Kevin was working in Glasgow and it would normally have taken him half an hour to get home, but that day he walked through the door within fifteen minutes. When I told him that Ally had been shot and was critical he never said a word. He just turned away and headed up the garden and went behind the garden shed. I knew he would cry away from me, as he has never been a lad to show his emotions in public.

There were two other people who meant the world to me, and I felt that I had to let them know what had happened. The first was my sister. She started screaming and pleading with me that the military had made a mistake and that it must be someone else's son, it couldn't be Ally. Her son was working in Iraq and was close to Ally. They used to go clubbing together when they managed to be on leave at the same time. I left her with the task of telling the family.

Next I phoned my dearest friend, Margaret Magill. We had been very close friends since meeting at the regiments' wives club when both our husbands had been serving. We have been great friends ever since, even after our husbands left the regiment. Ally's closest friend in the battalion was her son Matthew, or Matt as he was known. I had to get word to him before someone else did. Like the rest of us, Margaret took the news very badly. I felt guilty that I was leaving her to tell Matt.

Within an hour we had packed a bag and headed to Inverness, where the regiment was based, at Fort George. Alistair's wife Tracey phoned my daughter when we were about halfway there to tell us that Ally had survived the journey to another country but was critical. She said he had been assessed by a neurosurgeon and they would probably operate the following morning. That's when it registered with me that he had been shot through the head, and I started crying again. Not many people survive a gunshot through the head and I really thought then that he had very little chance of surviving.

The thought that my son was going to die in a foreign country with no family with him was more than I could bear. Tracey warned us that the Families Officer and the battalion padre would be in the house when we arrived, and not to panic as it was standard procedure. Captain Brian Johnston was the welfare officer - Frank and I remembered him from bygone days when Frank had served in the regiment.

After being introduced to Major Patterson we were told that the latest message received by the battalion was that Ally had been shot by a sniper and that the bullet had entered above his left eye and exited above his left ear. I thought at the time it might not be as bad as I first feared and that he would survive. Phillip became my saviour for the whole time we stayed in Inverness. We all prayed together for Ally.

Ally has a son called Owen who was only six. Tracey sat with him down and explained as best as she could that his dad had been hurt and was in hospital. Poor little Owen asked her if his dad was going to be OK and Tracey told him that she didn't know as he was very poorly. We made it through the first day, but none of us got much sleep.

The following morning we were all up at dawn after a long night. The back door opened about nine o'clock and Matthew Magill and his wife Jayne came in. My heart broke when I looked at their faces. It was obvious that they had been crying. When we hugged, we all started crying again.

We did something we were going to get used to - we made more tea and sat around the table talking and waiting for an update from Brian Johnston or C/Sgt John O'Neill from the welfare office. I'm sure we were all thinking the same and hoping Ally was still alive and was going to survive.

Some days the news was good and others it was not so good. Some days his temperature had risen, some days his heart rate was too fast, but at least he was alive. The surgeon operated on him three times in the first week to remove bone fragments from his brain.

Early one morning C/Sgt John O'Neill came to the door, and we all went into a panic thinking that it was bad news. He wanted Tracey's permission for the surgeon to perform a tracheotomy. For the next three weeks we went through so many emotions, praying that he would live and trying not to think of what damage had been done. By now we were aware that the bullet had gone in above his left eye and exited above his right ear, not his left, so we knew that the damage was a lot worse than initially thought.

We decided to keep a journal of the information we were getting told as I found that some details were forgotten because we were dwelling on other bits. I have read the journal once or twice, but found that the tears would start running again.

After three weeks the surgeon decided to reduce the sedation that Ally was getting to find out if his body would cope and whether he was stable enough to be flown back to the UK. Thank god he was holding his own. They decided to fly him into Birmingham on August 28 2006. The welfare team started to make arrangements to get Tracey, Owen, Frank and me down to Birmingham. We all travelled down on the day they were flying Ally home.

I had so many thoughts as we travelled down. I was glad that if the worst happened to him at least his family would be with him. Arrangements had been made for Tracy to stay in a hotel near to the accommodation Frank and I would stay in as there were injured soldiers staying in our unit and I think they wanted to save Owen from being exposed to adult conversations.

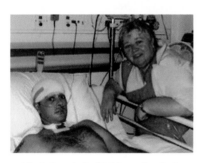
Ally in hospital with his mother Josie

Tracey felt very isolated being on her own with Owen.

The next morning Frank picked Tracey and Owen up and we were escorted to Queen Elizabeth Hospital by Michelle, one of the welfare staff, who did a fantastic job looking after the families of injured soldiers.

My heart was racing when Tracey and I went through the door of the critical care unit. Michelle had already been in to see Ally earlier and she tried to prepare us for a shock, but no one could have prepared us for what we saw. Because Ally had developed an infection similar to MRSA, they had him in the furthest corner of the ward, and as we turned the corner and came face to face with him we were stunned. Tracey was so shocked that she stopped and put her hands over her face and burst into tears. I got control of my emotions first and went back to her and led her to the side of Ally's bed.

Ally looked so big and swollen. He had slipped to the side of his bed, which had the safety guard up, and his eyes were bulging and the whites were yellow. He was staring at the floor. His head was heavily bandaged and we could hear his chest rattling as he was connected to oxygen through a breathing tube. He was connected to so many monitors that I wondered how he could have survived. His right hand had a white glove on which looked like a boxing glove. He had been trying to pull his lines out, so they had put it on him to prevent this.

When I think back to that day I remember him signalling with his head that he wanted the glove taken off, and when he had his fingers free he looked at me and made a signal that he was OK. He made an O with his finger and thumb and then held up his thumb. We asked him to blink to communicate with us and he did. He couldn't remember anything about what had happened, which I think was a good thing. That was a very emotional day for all of us; we all came out of that ward in tears. Poor Owen wasn't allowed to see his father, and I think that was just as well.

My son Kevin had a tough time when he saw him as they hadn't been on speaking terms before Ally went to Afghanistan. But Ally was never a vindictive lad and so Kevin got the same finger that it was OK. My daughter Louise sobbed and sobbed through her first visit to him and Matt and Jayne were the same, but as the days went by Ally got stronger and more tubes were being removed on a daily basis.

The surgeons operated on him again four days after he arrived at Birmingham. They asked to speak to us and explained that they had discovered a large abscess on his brain. They had drained it as much as they dared, as it was very close to his optic nerve.

A swab revealed that he had picked up tuberculosis. Although we had thought Ally was getting better, the doctors were very concerned about his infections and informed us that they were worried that if they couldn't get the infections under control he might not survive. It was another blow and there were more tears, to be told after all he had survived that he was still fighting for his life. He was having massive doses of antibiotics, three bags being drip fed into him at the same time. But Alistair being Alistair, he fought back and gradually started to improve.

Then one day when we went to see him we found he had been moved out of critical care into the neuro ward next door. He remained in isolation due to his infections, and was still receiving massive doses of antibiotics and being fed by a nasal gastric tube. The saddest part was seeing his left hand lying useless beside him, but within the week Nicky the physio came to start him on exercises. The first time they got him on to a standing frame and tipped up into the upright position the blood drained out of his face and he complained of feeling really sick. It had been almost six weeks since he had stood upright. He had good and bad days while he was in the QE.

We didn't tell him that a friend, Paul Muirhead, had been critically wounded three weeks after Ally had been shot. Paul died of his injuries a week after being blown up. His funeral was televised, and that was how Ally found out. I wish we had told him ourselves, as he became very distressed seeing it on telly.

The remaining lads came home from Afghanistan and within two days fifty of them came all the way down from Inverness to visit Ally. Their visit cheered him up no end and he talked about it for days. I thought he was a lucky man to have so many great comrades, many of them making the eight-hour journey down to visit him. His commanding officer, Lt Col Mike McGovern, and the RSM at the time, Nigel Bradley, came to visit him every six weeks.

At the end of October 2006 Ally was moved to Headley Court in Surrey, the military rehabilitation centre. Although he had made some improvements it began to dawn on Ally that his left side was paralysed due to the brain injury and he became very depressed, so much that at one point he said that if he could get to the window in his room he would throw himself out of it. His emotions were all over the place.

In February he was transferred to a brain injury unit back up in Birmingham.

In my opinion it was not the best place to put a soldier, as it was a civilian unit and Ally had nothing in common with any of the other patients, so he stayed in his room most of the time, only coming out for sessions in physio and meals. He remained there for nine months - he couldn't go home as his married quarter wasn't adapted for him.

When my son Kevin was down he mentioned that Ally could come home if we took the front door off its hinges, and that's what we did. Every weekend after that he came home, and his mood lifted so much. It was great to hear him laughing again.

A lot has happened since those days. Quarters were adapted for him and the battalion welfare arranged for him to come home every weekend. Sadly Ally's marriage broke up in 2008 and his wife went back to Scotland with their young son. It was hard to watch Ally come to terms with not seeing his son often.

When his wife phoned me and told me she was leaving Ally, my husband and I went down. We decided that as I wasn't working then I would stay and become Ally's full time career and Frank would travel up and down from Scotland to help wherever he could. He had carers coming in to get him up and dressed in the mornings and Ally did a lot for himself. He had to relearn a lot of skills that he took for granted before his injury, including going to the toilet on his own.

He went back to Headley Court in March 2008, and this time he was in a better frame of mind to try to get back some of the skills he had lost. When he had been there in 2006 he couldn't remember how to text. Now he was not only using his mobile but he had his laptop with him, and was even learning how to use PowerPoint again.

In 2009 he was moved again, to another brain injury unit near Headley Court, and he made a lot of progress in the two years he was there. He can now walk short distances with the aid of a crutch. We were told in the beginning that any improvements to Ally's condition would be very slow and I remember wishing that things would move a lot more quickly. But the people who deal with brain-injured people know what they're talking about. Things move at a tremendously slow pace, so I don't notice things changing.

Alistair finally left the brain injury unit in August 2010 and is now at home permanently. He attends physio in Shrewsbury Hospital and is lucky enough to have a very experienced physio who is making massive improvements

Alistair with his mother Josie and Father Frank

to Ally's overall mobility. He attends Headway twice a week and mixes with other people with brain injuries and enjoys their company. He also attends their woodwork class and enjoys the pub quizzes. After meeting a group of archers who had risen a lot of money for Help the Heroes Ally was invited to take the sport up himself and now trains twice weekly with a dedicated teacher, Pam Matthews. He can be seen out and about on his recumbent bike, and there's nothing he enjoys more that to go to some purpose-built trails with his former doctor and his mate Matt. They had a hard job trying to keep up with him as one of his former passions was extreme sports. He says the thrill of speed is not replaceable.

Alistair was finally discharged from the Army on the 29 July 2011. We are currently looking for a home for the three of us in Cheshire. It's been a long journey from that day the military rep knocked on my door. We have met a lot of fantastic people over the last five years, people we would never have met otherwise. We have cried oceans of tears.

We will soon leave the massive band of brothers and sisters we have met over the last five years, but we move on. Who knows what's ahead for Alistair? I will do my best to make sure he crams as much living as possible into the time we all have left together.

CHAPTER 6

AMBUSH - OPERATION HERRICK 8

DOMINIC HAGANS

In March 2008 the 1st Battalion the Royal Irish Regiment was deployed to Helmand Province, Afghanistan, as part of 16 Air Assault Brigade. The regiment had been given the task of training the Afghan National Army. We were known as the OMLT (Operational Mentor Liaison Team). Four Kadaks (battalions) of the ANA were to be trained by hand-selected men from each rifle company in the battalion. I was given the task of Company Sergeant Major, 4th Kadak.

During the tour each OMLT had 30-40 men selected to train and lead the Afghans into battle. Most of the Afghan soldiers were very courageous men, but at times they did let the OMLT lead and we were fighting most of the battles on our own with several of the ANA soldiers cowering.

My team had a very busy six months with the Afghans, from advance to contacts in the upper Gereshk valleys to the Kajaki Dam, the dreaded Marjah and down to Garmisir. The contact that stands out the most was the 360-degree ambush in Marjah.

On the morning of July 3 2008 we were on a routine patrol to Marjah. It was a lovely day and quite active with vehicle and personnel movement in and around the area. We were about 500 meters short of Green 1 and I was on the radio to let Cobra 0 know our position, when a family fled from a house, a man running with an old woman on his back. As we stopped to asses this my vehicle, which was at the front, was targeted by an RPG and a burst of automatic fire. The RPG missed, going over my vehicle, and the rounds landed in front, but we knew we were in an ambush.

We were surrounded and being hit from three firing points. We pushed forward, as my orders were to drive through. As we did so we were engaging all firing positions, and unknown to me Capt Beattie was being engaged from the rear.

As we pushed forward to Green 1 located in the green zone in Marjah (a green zone signifies friendly Afghan and ISAF occupation). I was followed by a Snatch Land Rover (an armoured Land Rover of the type used in Northern Ireland). I had pulled up in cover and started engaging the enemy, who we could see moving from cover in the woods and buildings. I sent an initial contact report, but we were on our own, with air support 45 minutes away.

I looked behind to see that all the ANA men had got

out of their vehicles and taken cover. They were now spread out up to 300 meters away with Capt Beattie stuck at the rear holding his own.

As the commander on the ground I had to act quickly. I ordered my gunner, Rgr Stewart, to give me covering fire, and then manoeuvered down the track for about 200 meters, which felt a lifetime. Rounds were landing all around me. I saw a Taliban fighter in a doorway 15 meters away, aimed my rifle and fired two or three rounds. He went down like a figure 11 target (those training targets with the image of a solider on them).

I pushed into dead ground and started shouting at the ANA to move down to Green 1 and stay in the river. Eventually I also got the ANA to move their vehicles, with the help of Capt Dougie Beattie, who was screaming at them.

Eventually Capt Beattie was able to get into a position to move up towards us. There was gunfire all around us and I could see in front of me the dirt being chewed up by the bullets from the Taliban. They knew I was there and I was a lone target for them.

I got the ANA men moving and more importantly enabled Capt Beattie to move. I ordered Rgr Stewart over the PRR (personnel role radio) to give me covering fire. I'm sure the Taliban could hear, because as I said that the amount of fire became heavier. I could see SSgt House, my medic, giving me cover as I tried to move.

I made a dash for it, heading back to my men, rounds landing around me. Then I felt something kick my left foot. A bullet had hit my boot, going straight through my sole - fuck me, how lucky was that!

I got back to my men and got us into all-round defence; we were now all at Green 1. We were now in a 360-degree ambush and pinned down. The Taliban had the advantage and we could see four or five in one firing position in the wood to the north-west.

We continued to engage with GPMG and 40mm HE grenades. I could see two enemy dead in the wood; they were moving rapidly around us, giving each other covering fire as they moved. This had obviously been well planned as they knew their ground well.

I tried to send an update on our situation as we lay on our belt buckles. I shouted at Cpl Brown, my driver, to get the TAC Sat antenna in the air, but as he did so it was shot out of his hands. There were two bullet holes through the antenna – fuck, no bloody comms! I knew Dougie had the spare, and he sent an update from his radio.

I looked over at Cpl Brown. His hands shaking and I remember him saying he needed a fag. What a time to ask. We were still taking heavy incoming fire and there were several RPG airbursts as well. The ground around me was like a fucking shooting range, rounds everywhere. Well, at least we wouldn't have to pick up the cases.

By the time the Apache arrived, I had to control our ammo as we were running low. We gave targets to the Apache and it was good to have it there, but the Taliban still stood their ground and fought.

To my west towards Green 2 I could see the enemy moving from the wood line to some buildings. To my south I could see the enemy using motorbikes to encircle us - we were surrounded. We needed a break. We had been there for two and a half hours and were still in all-round defence.

We needed to prove to the Apache who we were so we could strike the area of Green 2. The codeword was Boulevards, which we had to decode with our grid. It was sent, but spelt wrong, so the pilot declined.

At this stage I was well fucked off. I wanted to get me and my men out, so I went clear, gave our grid - fuck em, they weren't on their belt buckles with rounds landing around them.

Finally we got the Apache to engage Green 2, which gave us some relief at last. The enemy was fleeing as they were being gunned down by the guns in the sky. Dougie shouted 'Brummie, this is our opening!'

We got into our vehicles while the enemy was being taken on and I drove at speed towards Green 2, firing at two positions as we moved. 100 meters along an RPG was fired from my northern flank. It missed, but at the same time one was fired from the southern position which exploded at my bottom of my vehicle, ripping my door off. The door flew into the air and there was a big cloud of desert sand around me and my team.

The vehicle had stopped, and we got back on our belt buckles firing at the enemy. All the vehicles behind had stopped so we were on our own. I could see the enemy moving around Green 2, and we continued to engage them with our rifles. I put down a couple of HE 40 mm grenades. I couldn't reach the radio so I had to tell Dougie to get the Apache to take out Green 2.

The Apache let rip and there were clouds of dust everywhere – this was our break. We pushed forward at high speed, firing as we moved. The enemy was moving from building to building. My GPMG was rattling and the noise was deafening. As we went past Green 2 I could see four enemy dead on the floor - well at least we got them.

We approached Green 3, a small village with several shops. It was usually packed with shoppers and villagers, but now it was completely empty. The Taliban were using the village as cover. We were still being fired at, but I kept my foot down and went for it. At the rear Dougie was letting me know that everyone was keeping up.

When we arrived at the patrol base I could see the lads there in a fire position, covering us as we approached. I waited outside, giving cover as all my patrol came through. Finally I saw Dougie and his vehicle approach. We had made it with no casualties.

We moved inside and I paused for a while. How did we get out of that? Bad shooting from the Taliban or sheer luck? I didn't care, we were back. I checked my men, who were all fine, then sat down and sent a full contact report. I remember them saying 'well done'. Later a local elder reported that we had killed 18 Taliban fighters.

On this occasion the ANA faltered slightly and much of the fighting was carried out by the OMLT. At times the ANA can be good loyal fighters, but at other times they need the assurance of ISAF to help them out.

CHAPTER 7

OFFICER DOWN

MAJOR SIMON SHIRLEY

In 2008 I was commanding a mentoring team embedded within a battalion of the Afghan National Army in the town of Sangin in the Helmand river valley in southern Afghanistan. This necessitated us manning a series of quite isolated patrol bases, from which we would help the Afghans, dominate the area and interdict the Taliban. We were split into small teams of six to 10 personnel, so it was a lot riskier than most of the work the UK force does (most operate in groups no smaller than 30).

On April 6 my HQ team had responded with the Afghans to an attack on a police post that had left one of them dead and another injured. On conclusion of this, I took the opportunity to conduct an engineer recce of some of the patrol bases, as they needed serious improvement to their defences and living quarters. We had concluded visits to two of the bases and were driving south on Highway 611 (a glorified name for a rubble track) in a three-vehicle patrol led by my WMIK (open top Land Rover with machine guns mounted) with a Snatch Land Rover. My Sergeant Major was in another WMIK.

At approx. 1430 hrs the lead vehicle struck a landmine – an improvised explosive device. It was, to say the least, a peculiar experience. Usually in a sudden, violent event there is an anticipatory moment when your brain knows what is about to happen. When you get blown up, you don't.

I was launched into a whiteout similar to being trapped in big surf, except that it was dust and crap instead of water. Fortunately, I was wearing ballistic

Maj Simon Shirley's WIMIK after his mine strike - notice all the blood from his injuries.

goggles and therefore could have a quick peek at what had happened. I knew I would pull through as soon as I heard my driver, Cpl Chris Rushton; ask me if I was OK.

I had been pulling my machine gun to the left when we got blown up so my left arm was outside the envelope of the vehicle's armour. My goggles had been blown off and there was a lot of dust in my eyes, so I was limited in what I could see. However, my left hand was banging off my thigh and my initial thought was that there couldn't be much holding it on to my arm.

My Sergeant Major, John Cronin, was quickly forward and after a brief argument I accepted his opinion that most of my arm was still there. LCpl Sutherland, my medic, then did a superb job of dealing with my injuries: fucked left arm, shrapnel wound to the neck. After some dilly-dallying by the RAF, the helicopters eventually turned up and I was taken to our field hospital in Camp Bastion, where the surgeons worked on my arm for five hours to ensure I lost my argument with my Sergeant Major. Fortunately, the other guys in my vehicle were unhurt except for some hearing loss.

I moved to Birmingham the following day and had several operations on my arm and neck. I spent several weeks in Birmingham during my recovery. I was then moved to Headley Court to start my rehabilitation training, and spent several months there. I can't thank them enough for their dedication and the help they gave me in getting me to get back to some normality.

I eventually went back to work and resumed the role of a Company Commander at the Royal Academy Sandhurst.

CHAPTER 8

MAJOR SHIRLEY'S EXTRACTION

WO2 JOHN CRONIN

We had just left the ANA checkpoint, having conducted an engineer recce. Major Simon Shirley, Officer Commanding, was in the lead WMIK, the engineer Captain was commanding the Snatch and I was commanding the rear WMIK. We had driven about 100 meters when the OC's WMIK hit an IED.

I heard an almighty explosion and saw a large plume of dust and smoke. Time seemed almost to stand still. I grabbed at my radio and shouted 'contact, wait out!', but I heard nothing back. We were in a dead spot.

The engineer Captain was out of the Snatch, and I told him to try and establish comms with O (the main base in Sangin) as he had his radio man packed. I instructed the remaining soldiers to secure the immediate area. This had all happened before the dust cleared.

I looked towards the OC's (Officer Commander's) WMIK and could see the interpreter, Kadir, get out of the back. 'Don't move, stay in the wagon!' I shouted. I was concerned that there might be another device. Then I noticed Cpl Chris Rushton, the driver, get out of the driver's side and told him 'Chris, stay in the wagon!' But they were both in shock and couldn't hear me.

Sig 'Faz' Farrell was still in the WMIK manning the .50 cal. 'Faz, can you hear me, are you OK?' I shouted to him, but there was no reply.

I needed to get to the OC as I couldn't see or hear him. I handed over security of the immediate area to the engineer Sgt (Mac) so that I could clear a route to the OC's side of the WMIK. Kadir was now by my vehicle, so using the metal detector I followed his footsteps to the WMIK, clearing as I went.

Al, the medic, was behind me as I approached the passenger's side of the stricken WMIK. I looked at Major Shirley and saw that his face was covered in dust and blood. 'Sir, are you OK?' I said.

'I think I've lost my arm' he replied.

I looked at his arm and it was pretty mangled, I then looked into the footwell of the vehicle and could see that his legs were covered in blood. 'Shit, his legs are fucked' I thought. I asked him if he could move his legs and he replied 'yes'. Then I noticed a large hole in his neck. I opened the door and blood flowed out,

'Al, we'll have to get him back to the Snatch' I said. Al applied an FFD (First Field Dressing) to the OC's neck and together we eased him out of the WMIK.

'Fas, you OK lad'? I said to Farrell. 'I think so' he replied. 'Good lad, keep covering your arcs' I told him.

Cpl Rushton was now beside me. He was still dazed, but otherwise appeared unhurt. Al and I moved the OC to the side of the Snatch. The engineer Captain had by now established comms and informed O of our situation. The ANA, led by Capt Hazrat, were now at our location. I told him what had happened and asked him if his men could provide an outer cordon of security so that I could move my men into FOB Edinburgh, and he duly obliged.

Once Al had stabilized the OC we put him into the back of the Snatch with Al, Kadir and Chris. Then I went back and got Faz out of the stricken WMIK and put him in the Snatch as well. I closed the remainder of my guys in and briefed them that we would clear a route to the ANA FOB (Forward Operating Base, Edinburgh); the order of march was me on foot with the metal detector, then the Snatch, followed by my WMIK and then the remainder of the men on foot.

The ANA in FOB Edinburgh could see everything that had happened from their position, so they were ready when we got to the MEP. I was then able to establish comms back to Sangin DC (District Centre) (O) and inform the Ops Officer, Capt Martin, of the situation in full. I knew it was important to stay calm on the radio as getting frustrated wouldn't help matters.

I checked on the OC, Chris, Faz and Kadir. All except the OC were relatively unhurt, though Chris could hear ringing in his ears. After some time the Sangin QRF (Quick Reaction Force) arrived and the

OC and his men helped to secure the FOB for the helicopter's arrival. After about 90 minutes the heli arrived and took the OC away. A Viking call sign arrived and recovered the stricken WMIK into FOB Edinburgh. We stripped it of vital and secure equipment, then conducted a vehicle patrol back to Sangin DC, utilising the Viking call signs for protection.

Once I was back at the FOB, my main concern was that we had no Company Commander. But the 2i/c would step up, and my job was to keep the blokes' minds on the job and not worry about who would take over the company.

CHAPTER 9

SORRY SERGEANT!

RANGER ANDY ALLAN

I joined the army in March 2006 and embarked on six months' training in ITC Catterick. That September, when I had finished my training, I joined 1 Royal Irish in Inverness. For the first year and a half after joining the battalion I embarked on many exercises to get ready for the deployment. I was deployed to Afghanistan in

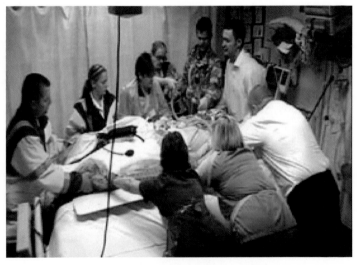

Back in Selly Oak in Birmingham, having lifesaving drills

58

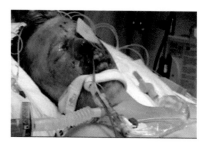

Andy in a bad way, battling infection

March 2008 and worked as part of an OMLT team training the Afghan army.

On July 14, while on foot patrol in the Musa Qala area, I was hit by an IED blast. The explosion ripped my right leg off and left my left leg in a very bad way and my eyes badly burned. When the dust settled Rgr Gavin Fox saw me lying in the canal in a bad way. He rushed immediately to my side and started administering life-saving first aid, while calling for Andy Kenny, the sections team medic, to help him.

My boss, Capt Meddings, was calling for help to get me extracted. Help arrived with Sergeant Benson; I remember saying sorry to all the boys and they shouted back 'Shut up mucker, you have nothing to be sorry for'. This is how friends take chances to help extract each other in the face of the enemy, with no regard for their own lives.

I was flown back to Camp Bastion by Chinook. Once I arrived the doctors and medics there carried out life-saving operations on me.

On the 16th of July I was flown back to the UK and then taken to Selly Oak Hospital, where I had my left leg amputated, as I was at risk of losing my life due to the severity of the damage and the risk of infection. I also underwent many other operations on my eyes and legs in the battle to keep me alive. I was sedated for seven weeks before I was gradually brought round.

I remember it all as if it was yesterday. My younger brother Christopher was there and I just kept telling him it wasn't my fault. About a week later my girlfriend Natalie, my sister, mum and stepfather came over I was never so glad to have my family around me and to hear that everything was OK with them, as Natalie was pregnant.

On October 7 I was transferred to Headley Court, where I began physio and got up on stubbies (temporary artificial legs). It felt great to be standing up, although it was quite hard as I couldn't see anything. I underwent intense fitness training and started a battle to try and gain my weight back, as I had lost so much while trying

After his recovery at Headley Court, training on his 'stubbies' before getting his new legs

to adjust to what had happened to me. I knew I had to gain weight so I could get home to see my family.

On November 19 my son Carter was born, I missed the birth as I was in the city hospital waiting to undergo an op to try and restore some eyesight. I arrived back in Northern Ireland on the 20th and was able to see my son as the op had restored some sight.

I'm still doing as much fitness and physio as my body will let me. I have had several more operations on my legs and eyes, I now can see my son more clearly now, thanks to the fantastic medical help I have received.

Andy With new-born baby Carter

I now live back in Northern Ireland with my family, and with their help I'm improving daily. I know I put loads of strain on them at times but that's what family is all about.

I guess I owe my life to many personnel from that day, but the main person I would like to thank is Rgr Andy Kenny for his fast action drills on the ground with the help of Rgr Fox - they kept me alive, Thank-you.

I have not returned back to work, and to be honest I probably never will, at least not with the army. I have been helping out with the Battalion Recruiting team in Northern Ireland.

CHAPTER 10

'BLOODY DAISY CHAINS' - RGR ALLEN'S EXTRACTION

SGT HUEY BENSON

At 0600 hrs on the 14 July 2008 we left satellite station North Musa Qala on a routine framework patrol, tasked to push north into TOWGI KELI. At this stage the FLET (forward line of enemy troops) was approximately 300m north, marked by a blue Iso container on the 837 northing, which was also marked on our maps.

There were two call signs out that day, A11 commanded by Capt. Meddings from the Anglians and A11D, which was my call sign. Moving north was pretty much an advance to contact at this stage, and both call signs consisted of 6 OMLT and 20 ANA.

As we moved north through the green zone through Shawruz, all seemed to be normal. A11 were on the eastern edge of the green zone as A11d pushed through the center. We crossed the FLET, keeping one call sign static as we patrolled north in bounds. A11 had gone firm to look into depth as we moved north.

It was at this stage that the ambush was sprung. A

daisy chain of 8 to 10 devices exploded, severely injuring Rgr Andy Allen, who was part of A11. At this stage we began to move towards the other call sign to assist. As we moved into the open we were engaged by small arms and PKMs (a Russian machine gun) from three firing points. This preventing us assisting as quickly as I would have liked.

Andy had been blown into the canal and his right leg had gone, with severe injury to his left. He had also suffered severe flash burns to his face and eyes.

Rgr Andy Kenny was the CMT (combat medic trained) for the patrol and luckily enough he was with A11, because at this stage my call sign was still in contact. A11D began to set the conditions in order to evacuate him to a predestinated ERV (emergency rendezvous). An ERV is a place on the ground selected as a prominent feature that can easily be identified by day or night. If we come under fire and receive casualties, everyone knows where it is and can move there. A squad of ANA plus the OMLT pushed toward each enemy position in order to suppress the enemy and if possible launch into an assault, or at least push them back. A buffer was created as well as possible by my call sign and the ANA.

From here we moved to secure and clear the RV (rendezvous) – we give out an RV to soldiers in orders before an operation, so they know where they are on the ground when they come to that part. More importantly, if they become separated from the patrol they know to move back to the last RV and the patrol will move back and pick them up. Once the RV was secure we pushed again back into the Green zone to A11 location.

When we arrived A11 had already started to move towards us carrying Andy through the movement corridor we had made. As we moved I began to send the MIST report and 9 LINER, with the remainder of the call sign controlling the ANA men carrying the stretcher.

As I spoke to Andy he kept saying 'sorry' over and over, saying that he had checked and wondering how he had missed the ambush. At this stage I think he could still see. He was carried on a lightweight stretcher over irrigation ditches and lower compound walls. As we arrived at the CAS exchange point two Warrior armored vehicles went screaming past, aiming to suppress and stop any follow up. A third Warrior pulled in, along with the doctor from the District Centre. A quick exchange was done and then they were gone.

When Andy was laid in the back of the Warrior he sat up, looked at me then down at this legs. He said 'Fucking hell, Shoey!' then lay back down. The injuries to his eyes came afterwards as blisters formed and became infected.

I later discovered that the first aid administered by Andy Kenny at the point of injury was the best the doc had seen, especially in those conditions. The speed of the operation and the sheer determination of every man in A11 and A11D saved Andy's life. I think an element of luck played a part, and that Andy was not supposed to go that day.

As the IED was initiated, the IRT (incident response team) was about to land in Sangin to pick up a D&V case. They were immediately re-tasked to Musa Qala. At the same time the resupply patrol from FOB Edinburgh to the DC was also just arriving, consisting of four Warriors along with dismounts (soldiers who had dismount from the Warrior to fight in battle). They had been with us two weeks before at satellite station north to reinforce the OMLT on a few ops. So little did we know at the time that all this was going on and making its way towards us? As the doc was finishing in the DC, the helicopter came in, so everything fell into place at the perfect time.

Once Andy had been extracted, bolstered with the dismounts and extra ANA soldiers that had made their way to us when they heard the explosion, we pushed north once again, clearing the area of remaining Taliban and securing the IED location to be exploited by ATO. They found a daisy chain of 10 devices with a 50m command wire had been dug in along the line of crops with a spider device on the end. The device itself had been dug in from inside the canal upwards, so there was no ground sign. The saving grace was that they had not dug them up far enough. Andy had been over the main charge, while the others luckily were between the other devices.

To this day I cannot believe that with the exception

of a few cuts and bruises and some damaged hearing, Andy was the only real casualty.

During the next few days all the guys could think about was how Andy was getting on. The fact that we are soldiers does not mean we don't have feelings. It's at times like this that we pull closer together and become more like family, so protective of each other. I guess that's why we call it the band of brothers.

CHAPTER 11

OPERATION HERRICK 13, 2010 - 2011

CAPTAIN TOBY WHITMARSH

A combat tour of duty in Afghanistan lasts no longer than six months and 21 days, but is preceded by an intensely demanding one-year period of pre-deployment training (PDT) and followed by a period of reflection which encompasses everything from televised award shows to an enduring and steadfast commitment to the family and friends of our fallen.

Some soldiers move on quickly to the next thing, and then the next, always staying one step ahead of any deeper introspection. At the other end of the scale, there are families living day to day who are working through feelings of loss and bereavement which only seem to grow with time. For all of us however, Afghanistan will remain a defining experience, a touchstone that we look back on with pride, some sadness and also a little amazement that we really lived through such times.

We began pre-deployment training with a new Commanding Officer (CO) and a new set of guiding principles. It was a time of optimism and urgency both within the battalion and in the army as a whole, as a fresh approach in Iraq and Afghanistan appeared to be paying dividends. The ubiquitous Taliban were reclassified as 'insurgents'. Our focus was no longer on the enemy but instead on an ambivalent population, worn down by the constant bloodshed, hungry for progress and understandably suspicious of our motives. The mission: to separate and protect the population from the insurgency, support the various strands of the Karzai government and further governance in a largely lawless area of Helmand Province. There was a school of thought that this concept might prove beyond our young rangers, but this proved completely unfounded. For months prior to the deployment, the battalion lived and breathed COIN (Counter-Insurgency). Accounts

The soldiers received a warm welcome from Afghan villagers

of the campaigns in Borneo, Malaya and Northern Ireland were dusted off and pored over for any detail that might prove relevant to the complex human terrain we were set to encounter. It was a salutary lesson that often when we think we are breaking the mould we are merely standing on the shoulders of our predecessors.

PDT demonstrated that 1 Royal Irish had taken COIN to its heart and was ready to take on the challenge of 'holding' a fiercely contested Area of Operations (AO). With few exceptions the training was an accurate reflection of what was to follow, and in its desperation to prove our readiness, both to the OPTAG (Operational Training & Advisory Group) Staff and our new CO, the battalion tackled every obstacle with total commitment. We knew all too well that if we failed to take on board the lessons we were being taught in the peaceful surroundings of Salisbury Plain or the Norfolk Broads, the result in a few months' time would likely be serious injury or worse. Yet by common consent, the greatest motivation was the fear of being found wanting; of not making the cut and getting spat out to the periphery of the battle group.

There was also another dynamic at work. A company had been warned that they would be going to a recently-augmented AO centred on a town called Saidabad on the border with Marjah District. Reports began filtering back of intense fighting and increasing ISAF casualties. Any prospect that this particular Afghan tour would be less kinetic than previous trips was now discarded. This would be counter-insurgency under fire against a determined and ruthless opponent. We were going to war, and unlikely to make it home unscathed.

The movement of a whole battle group with attached arms into theatre is an immense undertaking, but it was completed with the minimum of fuss and resolute good humour. The more experienced were quick to remind first timers brimming with nervous energy that there would soon be greater hurdles to face than a few more days of caffeine poisoning in Camp Bastion. Like Apache Scouts, our first soldiers had deployed to theatre more than a month and several thousand miles ahead of the main body. Without exception they became quickly embroiled in the Lancashire Regiment's battle rhythm, sharing in their fight and learning vital lessons that would prove invaluable to the Battle Group when it took over the reins at the start of October.

It was a great feeling when the first of three heavily-laden Chinooks disco-danced their way into our makeshift HLS outside Patrol Base (PB) Kalang. It was great to see the OC and the boys and recognise the relief in their faces that the waiting game was now over and what we had been working towards for nigh on a year could at last begin. Even the rounds bouncing off both the heli and the compound walls couldn't shake the mood.

There would however be no gentle introduction for 1 Royal Irish. The three days following handover were torrid and intense, the fighting vicious and often at close quarters. The first Op, Tora Karwan (The name given to the task of opening Route Devon so that A Company could be resupplied by road), saw A and C Company in continuous contact for more than twelve hours. There was also a civilian casualty incident straight out of the OPTAG playbook which saw the tiny PB transformed into a field hospital as six members of the local community were kept alive through the extraordinary efforts of our doctor and his determined band of team medics, most of whom had never seen a battlefield casualty before.

As A Company tried to navigate a path through the chaos threatening to envelope them, B Company found themselves fighting to protect the fledgling seat of governance. To lose this fight, or even take a backward step, raised the real prospect of mission failure before we had even really begun to make our presence felt. Those who were present maintain that the fighting was the most intense of the whole tour as the insurgents rolled the dice and made their play for the District Centre.

Once we had survived this initial trial by fire, nothing was ever so bad again. Getting through these first few days brought the battle group even closer together and forged a team ethic that would prove vital in the testing weeks and months to come. What could and (maybe should) have broken us had only made us stronger.

We felt a new confidence in the air. The Battle Group Headquarters (BGHQ) had proven rock solid under intense pressure and the companies had acquitted themselves magnificently in their first prolonged engagement with the enemy. At the same time we remained the learning and evolving organisation we had been in PDT – reassessing and honing our drills even in the heat of battle to better combat the insurgents next time around.

The first month was dominated by a series of highly successful 'pulses' carried out under the Tora Kanjak banner and dedicated to furthering our understanding of the AO. We called this process Find/Feel/Understand. These pulses included two air assault operations which projected combat power into areas previously considered 'no go'. These epitomised the CO's intent to prise the initiative away from the insurgents, utilising manoeuvre, mission command and ambitious, decisive planning. In American politics, they refer to it as 'the Big Mo', the irrepressible movement that can turn an also-ran into a president. In British military doctrine, it is known as 'tempo'. Once acquired, we were never to relinquish it.

Although October was a highly active month in which several casualties were sustained, key to our success was our ability to create a secure space in which we could begin our conversation with the people of Southern Nad-e-Ali. This was achieved through utilising our Operations Company and classic Air Assault tactics to mass force in in such numbers that we could temporarily 'lock down' whole kalays, map the human terrain, talk... but most importantly, listen.

Around these Battle Group Level 'Muscle Moves' the companies also carried out their own operations, such as Op Tora Basha 3, which saw B Company inflict a crushing defeat on the insurgent grouping that had previously dominated an area which Major Barron, the B Company OC, christened the 'Red Wedge'. And day in day out, the platoons in their isolated checkpoints put in the 'hard yards' providing their own solution to the question that dogged us in those early days of H13 and for which no OPTAG pamphlet had been written... just how do you conduct successful outreach when you are engaged within 50m of leaving your checkpoint? The answer was brutal in its simplicity and application - by assaulting firing points, by killing insurgents and never leaving the field of battle before the enemy did. The CO called it 'intimidating the intimidator'. Before we could tarmac roads and stock the local clinic we first had to win this battle. In this primitive part of the world the law of the jungle still reigned supreme.

On 8 November the Battle Group carried out Op Tora Zhemay (Black Winter) 1, the decisive act of which was the insertion of a new checkpoint, Tor Jan, in the 'Red Wedge'. The operation involved more than 300 members of the Battle Group and culminated in an outreach shura (meeting), hosted by the District Governor and attended by more than 180 local elders. It marked a tipping point for this strategically significant area. B Company, supported by the Operations Company, had established its dominance over the AO and inflicted a crushing defeat on the local insurgent network. The challenge now was to fully exploit this opening and create a new sense of linkage, both physical and psychological, between the community and their government.

For A Company November was perhaps our toughest month. The luck which had held in the early days of the tour seemed to lapse as we sustained a number of casualties. This was a product of our determination to keep the insurgent on the back foot by continually prodding and pushing him further away from the centres of population. Progress had been made, but we still oversaw a fractured AO with any move west to east impossible in daylight hours because of the number of enemy that continued to swarm into Saidabad from the ungoverned spaces on our flanks. Only at night could we traverse the AO freely and touch base with the multiples in Tanoor and Sabat. Typically we rendezvoused at Fourways Junction, tired bloodshot eyes and gloved hands meeting across the dusty track.

Rgr Aaron McCormick was killed by an improvised explosive device at dawn on 14 November 2010. Memories of this event will never fade, nor will the soul-searching that followed or the memory of typing up the simple, heart-breaking eulogies, written on scraps of paper and bits of cardboard.

For nearly two months we were under siege. We had only VHF radios with which to communicate and the most rudimentary security apparatus. Yet the insurgents were also under pressure, intelligence reports suggesting that they had sustained more casualties in the last three months than in the previous three years.

What would prove decisive in this war of attrition was our ability to 'change up', to mass force and dominate the ground to an extent the insurgents couldn't hope to match. It was therefore with great relief (and perhaps a sneaky regret that it was no longer our exclusive domain) that we watched the Delta Dogs saunter into the new improved PB Kalang. They were here to help us 'shape' the AO, in preparation for a clearance operation which would hopefully rid Saidabad of its enduring insurgent infestation for good. By shape, they meant to dominate the fiercely-contested ground in the centre of the AO, including the busy avenue where Sgt Keogh had earned a Military Cross the previous week. Like any experienced fighter, they would not go looking for the knockout blow from the first bell.

The confidence of our Operations Company was infectious. Thus far they had met with little but success, smashing through localised insurgent networks on a whistle-stop tour of downtown Southern Nad-e-Ali. Their command team brought fresh eyes to the Saidabad conundrum and a perspective unvitiated by painful losses and growing exhaustion.

Their sustained presence in the south began to reap dividends, and they quickly established a regular matrix of patrols in areas where there had previously only been fighting. Life gradually returned to a kalay which had until recently been a ghost town. Small shops began to spring up and the farmers returned to the fields, frantically working to make up for lost time. They established themselves in 'Divis Tower', a compound whose unusual second tier allowed for an all-seeing OP which dominated and becalmed the surrounding area. This was illustrative of the Afghan respect for visible security. Throughout the tour nothing proved more effective at reducing insurgent activity than the introduction of an observation point at a tactically significant location. There was always a fine balance to maintain; manning these static locations but at the same time not losing the ability to manoeuvre in strength. Contrary to received wisdom, we found that it was worth sacrificing a degree of force projection in the cause of a static checkpoint at the heart of a vulnerable kalay. In counter-insurgency perception is everything, and by placing ourselves physically within the community we were empowering people to reject the insurgency.

The problem with flooding an area is that the insurgents will often be unwilling to take you on. This may seem counter-intuitive, but key to 'shaping' the AO was drawing the insurgent on to the battlefield. This required inventive tactics and a degree of risk. It was vital to give the impression (real or otherwise) of vulnerability. One ruse involved setting off an enormous fake IED on a prominent junction. This netted a prominent commander who couldn't resist investigating what he hoped had been a successful strike on ISAF forces. The lesson was clear; to achieve real progress the cunning and ingenuity of the enemy must be matched.

By Christmas, Checkpoint (CP) Ranger had been established by the Dogs in the heart of bandit country. It was a powerful statement of intent, but only represented a job half done. The reality was that the Afghan army and police had thus far played only a limited role, and this had to change if we were to fulfil the brigade commanders' wider intent. This was because there were not enough of them in the A Company AO (Area of Operations). The police had no permanent presence and the ANA was confined to the western side of the AO, permitted to venture east for no more than two days at a time.

The solution as prescribed by General Petraeus was to generate localised counter insurgents, an Afghan Local Police Force (ALP) which would fill this security vacuum in the short term. The intention was to provide communities with the means to manage their own security in partnership with ISAF. The village elders would nominate prominent (male) members of their communities to be trained at a centralised facility, specially equipped for this purpose.

Unfortunately at this point things stalled, probably in hindsight because we were trying to direct proceedings according to our own concept of 'best practice' as opposed to thinking Afghan. The communities, still fearing Taliban reprisals and unwilling to venture far from their kalays, just would not commit. We were unfortunately not the only people who saw this project as a 'game changer'; the Taliban also saw its potential to transform the security picture in the south and did everything they could to undermine it, using their stooges on the district council to shout down proponents of the scheme and threaten anyone who expressed a willingness to join up.

Arguably the two key factors in getting the ALP off the ground were firstly the improved level of security, which lessened the fear of reprisals for such a visible repudiation of the Taliban, and secondly the introduction of a new training model which successfully took the mountain to Mohammed. Small training mentoring teams were dispatched to the different ALP locations, where they would fit and adjust according to the specific needs of that community. It was also a matter of good people as well as good policy. Pete Leckey and Dougie Beattie never gave up on the concept, even when it seemed to be going nowhere fast. The company commanders forged the personal relationships that would ultimately get us over the start line.

The Saidabad AO contained a prominent Hazara community centred on Saidabad Kalay itself. For years they had chosen the path of least resistance, left alone for the most part by the Taliban as long as they paid crushing taxes and shied away from openly practising their Shia faith. It was not much of a life and a huge waste of an educated and industrious people. On the few occasions when they had had the temerity to stand up for themselves they had been crushed by the local Taliban.

Huge efforts were made to secure this vulnerable minority, including the introduction of three new observation points to dissuade any insurgent infiltration. This worked to the extent that for the first time in living memory the Hazaras felt able to openly practise their faith, free from reprisal. Yet what they really lacked was leadership. Their representative on the District Council (DCC) had been killed in a hellfire strike while attending a Taliban shura and his son (the prospective candidate) seemed determined to maintain the family tradition of working with the Taliban as a means of safeguarding his position.

For their part, the Hazara elders referred to Asadullah Karimi as their de facto leader and the only person who could authorise Hazara participation in the ALP. The complicating factor was that he no longer lived in Saidabad but in exile in Herat with a Taliban price on his head. Eventually he did return under ISAF protection, becoming the interim DCC Member and overseeing the introduction of a Hazara ALP. A giant among his people (both in personality and size), he was a ruthless, brazen negotiator and notoriously unpredictable. Nevertheless one could not fault his bravery in facing down a fatwa which would never be rescinded. He died much as he had lived, striding from his compound to remove an illegal Taliban road-block some months after we left Helmand.

The other two Pashtun elders were in their own ways equally courageous and having started on this path it was our duty to stand shoulder to shoulder with them. Our commitment to this project was not universally popular. Some said the ALP was nothing more than a militia, a means for local elders to feather their own nests, and that we should be concentrating solely on developing the Afghan Uniformed Police (AUP). However those actually in the arena were not only determined to honour a commitment to people we regarded as colleagues and friends but also painfully aware that this was the only game in town.

Sustainable, intuitive and distinctly Afghan, it was our best answer to an age-old stumbling block; that an insurgent with a mobile phone can defeat a whole Infantry Company provided his threat is conceivably genuine. By arming, training and supporting what amounted to neighbourhood watch schemes, we helped develop within our sponsored communities a new resilience and gave the lie to the insurgents' boldest claim – that they could reach any member of the local community who had the temerity to stand against them.

Tor Zhemay III ended on the 14 January 2010. It had lasted 57 days, and felt more like an odyssey than a military operation. The statistics say it all: 500 troops involved, 131 patrol contacts and 22 enemy attacks on checkpoints. More than that, however, the entire security infrastructure was transformed. Six new checkpoints (including CP Ranger) and four new observation posts were built in locations where they would best protect locals and shut the Taliban out. Poorly positioned checkpoints were simply shut. To get this done required sending 614 lorry loads of aggregate down two of the most dangerous roads in Helmand to wherever 51 Parachute Sqn were hard at work. The result was a combustible mix of insurgents looking for easy targets, dodgy security guards, Afghan security forces of every denomination and our own patrols on the ground fighting to protect the population and keep the wheels turning. At times it was chaotic, dirty and dangerous, but out of this melting pot came something of lasting significance. The reality is that you cannot 'clear' an area in a couple of days, let alone secure a population. You have to get into the weeds of a place and its people, exposing yourself to risk and doing the basics well, day after day, patrol after patrol. It is the only way you will earn trust. It is the only way to defeat insurgents who don't own watches.

To consolidate our advantage the battle group now switched its primary focus away from the main population centres and looked outwards. The insurgency was down but not out. It would look to regroup, possibly to launch a fresh summer offensive. Our objective now was to find and finish. In A Company our focus was on Zaborabad, where we believed the remaining insurgents were holed up and awaiting our departure. It was also time to increase the extent of our engagement with 2/9 USMC (United

States Marine Corps) and the cross-boundary areas that the insurgents had quickly identified as our limit of exploitation when pursuing them post-contact.

Even as the weather deteriorated and the patrol base was reduced to a quagmire, we maintained our tempo of patrolling and pushed forward with fresh initiatives designed to incentivise the reporting of IEDs. Unfortunately however the company was hit hard by the death of Rgr Dalzell in an operational accident. It was a tragic loss of a young man whose dedication to his fellow rangers and bravery in combat belied both his youth and the roguish tales he would spin out, to the delight of his muckers in Checkpoint Ranger. It is perhaps still too raw to talk about how the Dalzell family and the battalion faced up to this awful event; suffice to say that there is no one touched by this incident who does not respect and admire the compassion and dignity shown by the Dalzells.

The last major operation of Operation H13 was Tora Zhemay IV, which involved more than 300 soldiers inserting in a single aviation wave into Zaborabad. The intention was to project overwhelming force into an area that was still utilised by insurgents as a launch pad for operations, north into the District Centre and south into Marjah. 'A' Company were the outer cordon, positioned to mop up insurgents attempting to extract from the area.

In statistical terms the operation was a slam-dunk, with fourteen separate finds of weapons, IED components and ammunition. More significant however was the psychological impact of the operation on the local population. There had for some time been an active ISAF presence in this area, but this uncompromising show of strength provided the decisive breakthrough. In a subsequent shura local elders, not usually noted for either bravery or memorable sound-bites, for the first time publicly repudiated the insurgency. They subsequently stood by this commitment and the area was almost completely becalmed for the rest of our time in Helmand.

There was still however unfinished business with the ALP. It was now a living, functioning entity, though crucially not ratified by the Ministry of the Interior and therefore illegal. The complexities involved in establishing the consensus required would drive anyone to madness; luckily Pete Leckey was that way inclined long before he had ever heard of the ALP. The setbacks were endless, the political machinations completely mind numbing, but worse was the sheer inertia displayed by certain individuals who refused to countenance the possibility that this was neither a vanity project nor an effort to detract from the existing security apparatus.

As a result the stumbling blocks just kept coming. The initial weapons supplied by the AUP were woeful and prospective 'Mohali' police were required to complete a twenty-page document (not easy when you are illiterate) and prove their citizenship. Separate to these annoyances however was a tragic incident that threatened briefly to derail the whole enterprise. The nephew of an ALP elder was travelling in a vehicle which sped through an ISAF cordon and was justifiably engaged by soldiers convinced they were under attack from a suicide bomber.

It is easy to become cynical in a country where grief can often be assuaged by compensation, yet in this instance the hurt was genuine and heartfelt. That the ALP did not melt away back to their compounds is a tribute to the unshakable bond that had developed between the C Company OC, Ally Harbison, and the ALP Commander, Sardar Mohammed.

Our relief at seeing the ALP formally ratified by the Afghan Ministry of the Interior and accepted as a key part of the district's security apparatus was tempered by our frustration that we would soon be handing our roles over to people who we worried would not match our commitment. These concerns were legitimate, as the ALP was a frequently misrepresented concept and not universally popular. We needn't have worried however, as 45 Commando were straight into the trenches alongside us. Full immersion followed. They sat in on every shura, read every email, pored over every file and in quiet moments sat back with a brew and just listened. A larger than life tale of betrayal, courage, setbacks and sacrifice. Leckey, chief storyteller, waxing lyrical yet again. Osmosis, indoctrination, call it what you want. They had to feel it the way we did. The moral component of their fighting power.

Outside our little Shawquat world, with only weeks and then days remaining in theatre, the companies continued to pursue the remaining insurgents. 'Safe haven' was now a derelict term. The Delta Dogs had pushed out to the furthest corners of the AO to ensure that there would be no 'fighting season' in 2011. To rest on our laurels at this stage would have been easy, but also a stain on those who had sacrificed so much to get us to this point. We owed it to them to finish the job we had started.

It was in the fulfilment of this obligation that LCpl Stephen McKee lost his life as a result of an IED strike on his vehicle. He was universally popular and the regiment coursed through his veins. It is perhaps some consolation that he died doing the job he adored, shoulder to shoulder with people who loved and respected him unreservedly.

In those last weeks, Jamie Humphreys and 'A' Company would regularly patrol from the Bolan T Checkpoint in the West to the Neb Canal in the East and everywhere in between. In October Sgt Hanthorne's multiple had fought for their lives less than 20m from PB Kalang, pinned down behind the deserted stalls of a bazaar shut on Taliban orders. On their final day prior to handover this bazaar opened for business once again, the threats meaningless because those who had issued them were either dead or in exile. In our last week in NDA(S) there was one kinetic incident. 45 Commando Battle Group were to have four in their whole deployment. In six hard months the Company had battled through 471 engagements with the enemy.

The victories and symbolic achievements seemed to flow thick and fast in our last month in theatre, like a dam that had finally burst following a vast and prolonged accumulation of pressure. Their effect was to briefly anaesthetise the battle group against the painful losses that we had suffered and memories of times which we would rather forget. Yet almost a year down the line, the parades and celebrations a dimming memory, our commitment to the families of the fallen remains resolute. We will not forget.

Yet as a regiment we must also move on. Herrick 13 is now almost a year behind us and there are big, serious, and exciting challenges ahead, most notably a battle-group level exercise in Kenya and a possible deployment somewhere in 2013, which will likely be as different to H13 as it was to H8 and H4, and no less demanding as a consequence. The reality is that there is only ever one tour worth talking about... the next one.

CHAPTER 12

ONE FALSE STEP

CPL PHILLIP 'BARNEY' GILLESPIE

I have wanted to be a soldier for as long as I can remember. When I was growing up my dad told me about my mother (who had died when I was one year old) who had served as a radio operator with the Green Finches. This was at a time when there were few women in the British Army and a tour in Northern Ireland meant facing significant conflict. My mother's legacy and courage have been my motivation all along. I have worked hard (top student at Catterick completing full RSJ and SCBC), because I love what I do and have had continuous support from my girlfriend, father and brother back in Northern Ireland.

As soon as I could, I trained with the Army Cadets from 12 years old until I was eligible to enlist as a regular with the Royal Irish in 2005. I am now 23 years old, a Corporal and with three tours of Afghanistan under my belt (2006, 2008 and 2010). My plan was to progress on to Sergeant as soon as possible.

Suddenly, thanks to an IED, I find myself with a new

life course, planning my future without my right leg and with complex multiple fractures in my left leg. This is my personal story about my injury and my recovery over the last six months. It is an experience you can't make sound good, because it just isn't. It's hard. However I have learned from my family the importance of not getting bogged down in asking the question 'Why this did happen to me?' There's no point. It's just spilt milk. It will not help in my recovery; in fact it will probably slow things down.

I suppose I would describe myself as someone who combines being laid back with a strong sense of professionalism and pride in what I do. I have slowly earned the respect of peers from following through on actions and working hard. The army has taught me this and given me the unique opportunity to push myself. On many occasions I have been forced to step out of my comfort zone. I have always been surprised by what can be achieved. All that experience was good preparation for this one.

I was injured on the morning of 9 January 2011, twelve weeks into the tour. It was a freezing Afghanistan morning and I was my usual reluctant self, crawling out of my camp bed under the poncho. Ironically, as with all things in life, the sequence of events that led up to me starting as 'point man' that day was a series of random last-minute changes of strategy and miscommunication. As normal I put on my body armour and my helmet (for luck I keep two gift cards from my father and brother tucked into the helmet lining.) I scoffed the unrecognizable all-day breakfast and we headed out on patrol.

One of the hardest lessons I have learned from being injured was not to ignore my gut feelings. I won't make the same mistake twice. I just knew something wasn't quite right when I took the route I did. A few moments later, I stepped on the pressure plate of an IED.

The bang was massive, with a blinding light. After a couple of seconds I partially came to, and remained conscious. For a moment I thought it was just my mate Scanners who had been injured – he was temporarily blinded by the blast.

I checked over my body and saw that my right foot had gone and my calf muscle looked like it had been put through a mincer. My shin bone was like a bone hanging out from a piece of meat. It was all very strange.

Initially I felt no emotion. I just thought about the drills I had learned and what needed to be done, and shouted for help. A few seconds later several new thoughts went through my head - my girlfriend would leave me or never go away with me, I was never going to be able to drive again, my army career was ruined, life was never going to be the same. I was right there.

Within seconds two of my colleagues were working on me. My mate Kevin, who I had known all my life, risked running over to be with me. I remember being worried for him because of the sight of my leg was so shocking.

Shortly after other guys from my company all came over, risking their lives from secondary devices, including the CSM. The feeling I got from knowing they were there until the casevac team arrived is difficult to put into words, but I felt so supported. The medical teams worked like Trojans and were fantastic. They put me out and I don't remember anything else till I woke up in Camp Bastion.

I believe the time from being injured to getting to the hospital was around 45 minutes. I learned afterwards that the swiftness of my extraction was also down to the professionalism of the 2 i/c, who without any hesitation stepped up to manage the process. I was also told that another colleague, Tam, also came to help me as soon as he heard the news over the radio. He stayed with me till I was put on the MERT, and was the last person to say goodbye. People's gut reactions that day really moved me.

By chance one of my best mates, Ally, was also around and he stayed with me for more or less the whole time until I was flown back to the UK.

You can't underestimate what army mates do for a guy who has just lost his leg. Instead of feeling miserable, we laughed and joked and had a bit of crack until I got separated from Scanners, who was in the bed next to me. He told me in true army style 'Barney, I can't see you at the moment but I can smell you from here!'

For punishment, the medical staff ended up delaying my return, saying I was well enough to wait because there were other more urgent casualties. When I got to the hospital in Birmingham my father was there, and he did not leave me the whole month I was there. My girlfriend gave up the job she was doing and came over, and my brother was also very supportive. Losing your leg changes you and affects the people around you, it's a fact. When I first saw my girlfriend and family it was one of the most emotional times of my life. I didn't show it on the outside as I didn't know how they would react, but we had a very strong connection as a family that day. I could see the relief on my Dad's face that I was still alive.

When I was discharged from the hospital for two weeks my girlfriend cared for me round the clock - she was amazing. It was such a change having to get up four times in the night, dealing with the phantom limb pains, and all the time she only moaned about my hair and sideburns.

As I write this I am into my second admission at Headley Court, where I go every four weeks for a month. Rehabilitation is a series of gains and setbacks, then more gains and more setbacks. It's just the way it is. I now have to have further surgery to my stump, but within a few weeks I will be back on my prosthetic leg and walking and running again. Saying it like that may make rehabilitation sound easy – it certainly is not, its bloody hard work. But it's much easier with the help I have received from my girlfriend, family and friends and my unit. They give help in the form of taking time to put things in places I can reach and stay independent, putting the dog outside so he doesn't jump on me, having a homecoming party in my home town with all my extended family and friends there. This was another example of how much people cared and just made it all easier to cope with.

I want to stay in the army if I can, but I don't know what is going to happen - I suppose none of us do. I can't say yet for sure how losing my leg has affected me, but I am planning a holiday with my girlfriend already and am back driving my car. I am determined not to let having a prosthetic limb stop me doing things. I just need to plan and think more.

CHAPTER 13

MY BEST MATE'S DOWN -
BARNEY GILLESPIE'S EXTRACTION

CPL TAM DOWIE

We had been in CP Divis (so called because the stag (sentry) position on the roof resembled the Divis flats in Belfast) for about four weeks, providing security to the build and construction of PB Ranger. Before this Barney Gillespie and I had been in the same multiple Wildcat, two zero - we worked together as the dreaded Vallon men, operating mine detectors. We were both experienced NCOs with two previous tours of Afghanistan in the bag. Coming as we did from the illustrious Reconnaissance Platoon, it didn't really faze us.

When we moved into Divis all three Wildcat multiples broke down into sections, with the likes of Barney and me taking it in turns to be section commanders on the ground along with the other NCOs in the Top Heavy D Coy (the Company was over the top with certain ranks in it). Some days you could be a section commander and other days you'd be carrying the ECM (Electronic Counter Measures equipment) or doing point man, so we were definitely kept on our toes.

Some NCOs might say that full CPLs like Barney and me shouldn't be carrying ECM or doing point man, but we were recce soldiers and we all took our fair share of the work and set the example for the junior blokes.

On the day Barney was injured I was on my guard day, the rotation being two days on patrols, one day guard, which was a kind of admin day. I had just come off stag in the ops room and lain down on my bed when I heard the explosion. I knew it was our boys as I'd closed the gate behind them as they left the CP. Barney was point man for his section that day and as always I had told the boys to stay safe.

I jumped off my bed with that horrible gut-wrenching feeling you get when you know one of your own has been injured. As I headed into the ops room I heard Sgt Scanlon (the section commander for Barney's section that day) send a contact report: 'four zero, this is Wildcat two zero bravo contact IED'. My gut-wrenching feeling got worse and I was weak in my legs, because as Sgt Scanlon finished the report he let out a horrible painful whimper.

I immediately grabbed my rifle and headed for the gate of the CP. The boss, the medic and a couple of the other guys followed me and we ran as hard as I could towards the sound of the explosion. On our way we made sure we cleared the way to the scene by using our Vallon mine-detection kit.

On arrival I ran into the casualty RV party leader, Rgr Templeton, who informed me that we had 2 Cat A casualties but he didn't know who they were. I looked towards the casualties and didn't want to believe what I was looking at. Scanners lay to my right and Barney to my front, with Jenga the medic and RGR Coulter tending to him. I still wasn't sure it was Barney at this point as his face was being covered by Jenga.

I asked Scanners if he was OK, and he said he was. I then moved to Barney, and couldn't believe my eyes or even want to believe them. He was lying there screaming at the top of his voice. He was in enormous pain. His right foot and ankle had been completely evaporated by the blast, up to about half way up his right shin. I could smell that horrible smell of burned flesh and blood.

I took Barney by the hand, and he looked up at me and said 'I'm fucked Tam, I'm fucked.' I wanted to cry, but I knew that if Barney saw me cry or flap in any way he might think he was worse than he actually was and go into shock. I knew in my heart that he wasn't as bad as some casualties I'd seen in the past, but I knew that if the medic monged it in any way Barney could lose his life.

I couldn't show my fear to Barney in any way, so I just told him he was all right. I explained his injuries to him and told him he was going to make it, no problem. I told him he'd be home with his girlfriend and family in a week or so.

I still had that horrible feeling. I still wanted to cry, because here was my mate lying on the floor with his leg off. It brought back memories from Herrick 4, when friends of mine had been killed.

I wanted to help Barney as best I could, so I just kept reassuring him that he was going to be OK and he'd be home with his missus soon enough. I told him he'd be taking her to New York for Christmas next year. He must have believed me, because he settled down a bit then and stopped complaining about being fucked. He asked where the MERT was, and I just kept telling him it was close and would be there soon.

We got Barney on the stretcher, the Chinook landed and the casualties were taken away. I shook Barney's hand, gave him a hug and told him I'd see him at the end of the tour and we'd get a drink then.

We got off the chopper and started back towards the contact point. As the chopper took off a wave of emotions took over me - anger, hate, rage and frustration. I started to cry. My boss, the CSM, Billy Roy, and a few of my mates tried to comfort me, but I didn't want comfort I wanted to be left alone to vent my anger.

I walked back to my CP with the rest of the lads in patrol formation, but I couldn't concentrate - I couldn't get my mind on the job. I got back to Divis and had a shower I felt numb all day. I really wanted to speak to my wife, but I knew I couldn't as OP Minimise would be on.

I tried to sleep but couldn't. I just lay there. I hardly slept that night and as soon as Minimise came off I rang my wife and told her what had happened. She cried as much as I did, as Barney's girlfriend Kirsty was her best friend and she didn't even know how bad Barney was - she just knew he'd hurt his leg. My wife called her after I'd finished on the phone with her and told her exactly what had happened.

As the days went by we got more and more snippets on Barney and Scanners. They were doing fine - they were even taking the piss out of each other. It made me feel better that Barney hadn't lost his sense of humour.

When I got a chance to call him and have a chat, I was really taken aback at how normal he sounded. That was a great relief. We took the piss out of each other, and he was eating a KFC as we spoke. I even told him I was jealous. We kept in good contact throughout the rest of the tour, taking the piss and having a laugh. He kept me well informed on how he was progressing and believe it or not he was walking before we got home from the tour. Three short months and he was on his feet.

He was even there for us when we got back, and it was good to see him standing there on the parade square. I gave the big man a hug and we went to my house and had a BBQ and got pissed.

Now as Barney recovers more and more, he comes and stays at my house on weekends and we have a drink and a laugh. I still hate the fact that my mate has lost his leg to a Taliban bomb, but as Barney says 'It is what it is and I may just get on way it', which is only too true.

CHAPTER 14

OH NO, NOT ON MY FIRST TOUR!

RANGER AARON NIXON

I'm Aaron Nixon and I come from Northern Ireland. I joined the army at 17 in 2007 and started my training to join 1 Royal Irish at the famous Infantry Training Centre, Catterick. It was a six-month course with a Scots company, where my platoon was known as Scots 2. It broke down into two phases. The first was basic army training, doing drill and weapon handling fitness etc, and phase two was trade training, which for me was infantry, so we did more training, such as things like FIBUA (Fighting In Built Up Areas).

After I passed out of the Infantry Training Centre in July 2008, I joined my battalion, which was already on Herrick 8 in Afghanistan. But because I was still 17 I wasn't allowed to deploy out to theatre. Instead we were sent to Cyprus for two months as staff for decompression (there's a place in Cyprus where troops coming back from a tour of Afghanistan can relax and sort their heads out before moving back to see their loved ones after a long time away). We spent most of the time doing guard and odd jobs about the camp and down on the beach.

Once the battalion got back from tour and after POTL (Post Operational Tour Leave), I was put into a company. After a while in a company, I got lucky and was put on to a specialist operative course, which was a week's pre-course then phase 1 and phase 2. I did the pre-course, but then a company went to Kenya to do enemy (role play as enemy forces), for two Scots who were doing their exercise there. We spent seven weeks around Kenya doing different serials as enemy for them and we also did a week's live firing company training.

When we came back from Kenya, CSgt Eddis, who was the Specialist Coordinator at the time, asked me if I would like to come and do phase 2 of the course, which was in Otterburn for five weeks, and I said yes. We learned a whole load of skills. We did the badge tests and I passed those OK. Now all I had to do was phase 1, which I did around six months later in Bisley, with a week's field firing in Brecon, where we stayed in Sennybridge. By this time PDT (pre deployment training) was starting, so we did all the training exercises and lessons leading up to deployment on Herrick 13. I got attached to B Company with Sgt Alvin Stevens CGC (he was awarded the Conspicuous Gallantry Cross for his actions during Op Herrick 8) as the Specialists for that company. When we got into Bastion and during RSOI (Reception Staging and Onward Integration) training we were told that we would be going to a checkpoint in Nad-e-Ali called Catina, but I got moved to a new checkpoint called Shingul. The checkpoint commander there was Sgt Adam Punyer and it was a D company multiple in B Company's area of operations. We went by Chinook and got dropped out to B Coy's Headquarters FOB (forward operating base). Here we were the only multiple to be moved into the checkpoint by mastiffs that night.

The first few days in Shingul were quite slow. We were patrolling and not much was happening, but after a few days it all kicked off and we were in contact every patrol, and on to the Sangers every day. After a while B Company's Officer Commanding wanted us to move up the road to CP Masaroof to get a rest from the fighting, but on the morning of the move it was postponed by 24 hours so instead we went out on patrol at about 6.45 in the morning. For this patrol I was doing point man with the Vallon.

We stopped at a small crossing point, where Pete Mawhinney and I went forward to clear the crossing and check for any IEDs. At this point we got engaged by small arms, and the first burst of rounds came at me and Mawhinney.

Suddenly I felt the impact of a bullet. A 7.62 mm round had gone through my thigh and my femur. I fell to the ground and dragged myself into a ditch. Blood was pissing everywhere and I was in agony.

The ditch was full of water, so I held myself up on the bank and called for Chris the medic to come over.

Mawhinney and the rest were keeping suppressive fire going down on the Taliban. Chris came over with covering fire from the men and jumped into the ditch with me. He put a tourniquet on my leg, followed by an FFD on the exit and entry wounds on my leg. Then he gave me morphine.

While everyone was suppressing the enemy, Adam was putting up the mist and 9 liners for Casevac. Once the MERT was on its way they moved me across the road into another ditch to wait for the MERT team, which was arriving under the escort of an Apache. Finally it landed and I was put on to it. The medics cut all my clothes off and put me to sleep. I awoke at 1430 hrs in the medical center in Camp Bastion, not knowing what the fuck was going on. I had a big metal frame on and was in pain, but I was alive.

My first operational tour was over, and so for the time being was my active service career. I was heading to England tomorrow to have further surgery at the new Queen Elizabeth hospital in Birmingham.

The next day I was aeromeded to Selly Oak Hospital in Birmingham, where I was taken straight into theatre again to get metalwork positioned in my leg to stabilize and straighten my shattered femur. It was only in Birmingham that they noticed I had an infection from the dirt and water called acinetobacter, which was deep in my bone and muscle. I was in and out of theatre quite a lot while they tried to get my leg clean and infection free, so it would have the opportunity to start healing.

But for around five weeks I was stuck in bed, unable to move with the pain. I had a suction pump on my leg which was constantly taking out pus and bits of infection. Thanks to the infection I was in Selly Oak Hospital for 25 boring weeks, but the welfare team made my life easier by bringing in things for me to do and taking me out on day trips when I was allowed.

I was eventually told what had happened to my leg. The bullet had entered the back of my leg, passed through and shattered my femur, leaving around five inches of my femur missing and a hole the size of your fist at the front of my thigh.

As for my career in the army, I was not really serving long enough to get it started, but what I have achieved so far I have loved, and I would have loved a long career in the army. I hope one day I will return to full-time work and put my uniform back on, but like many others it all depends on my recovery.

CHAPTER 15

POINT MAN DOWN –
THE EXTRACTION OF RANGER NIXON

RGR PADDY GUY

I was in Aaron's multiple in CP Shingul; we were part of a D company multiple which was working as part of B Company in Nad-e-Ali, Helmand province. We had heard all the rumours about Shingul before we had got there as it was a new checkpoint in an uncharted area in the AO. We all knew each other well, which was a great thing and made us click and work together really well; Aaron was our Specialist and he was the best. We were due to be relieved from Shingul on the 17th of October, but none of us were happy with this as we all enjoyed the amount of action we had been getting there and the guys had made it home for themselves. But that day we were told it would be put on hold for 48 hours for us to move to our new patrol base.

On the morning of the 18th of October at around 6 am I was sitting with Aaron and Pete Mawhinney and getting a photo taken of us before our last patrol. None of us looked impressed at all. We patrolled out and across the road and up the side of the canal which ran parallel to Shingul. Aaron was our point man, with Pete behind him and then our commander and boss Sgt Adam Punyer. I was at the back of the patrol with Jason Orr.

We all stepped into a ditch and went firm, as the footbridge we wanted to cross ahead looked suspicious. Aaron and Pete got out of the ditch on their own to check the bridge out and Vallon up to it. It was riddled with high metal readings, which slowed the whole process up. The Taliban had dug batteries and metal into the ground to get this effect.

All of a sudden there was a huge burst of gunfire. I remember looking up and seeing Aaron on the ground and Pete standing over him returning fire directly at the enemy. Jason and I moved up to the front of the patrol, got into another ditch and started to return fire. While this was happening Chris Shivas, our medic, moved to the front as well. We were lucky to have Chris as he is regarded as the top medic in 16 Brigade.

While we gave covering fire, Chris was able to move Aaron into cover and treat him. Aaron had been shot through his leg and the wound was very substantial, as the round had completely destroyed the bone inside his leg. Adam was trying sort out the helicopter casevac for Aaron and Jay Ennis, our MFC (Mortar Fire Controller), called in mortars to hit the enemy position. The rest of the patrol got around Aaron and got him on to a stretcher. Pete, Jason, Jay Ennis and I crossed the canal, which was chest deep with dirty, stinking water and a nightmare to cross. We placed ourselves in all-round defence for the helicopter's protection. It came in hard and fast on its approach.

I can remember the guys getting Aaron out and carrying him on to the chopper, still under fire. The four of us returned fire as the boys got him into the back of the Chinook, and seconds later it was away. I don't think it had hit me what had happened while we were out on the ground. I just concentrated on getting Aaron out of there.

We returned to Shingul, dumped our kit and got into some dry clothes. Pete and I had shared a room with Aaron, so it was weird not to have him around for banter and a laugh. Adam sat us down to see how we all were and ask everyone how they felt. Looking back at it, we all realised Chris's evaluation of the injury was 100% correct and he had done the perfect job of treating it. Pete's bravery in standing and protecting his friend had saved Aaron's life. The boys all really stepped up that day and did an amazing job.

None of us were able to contact Aaron for a few weeks after we had moved to our new base at Masaroof. It was great to talk to him and get an update on how he was, and as usual we took the mick and had a laugh with him. Throughout the remainder of the tour we all kept in regular contact with Aaron, and on returning to the UK we were able to get him up for our night out and catch up. Looking back on it, it was overwhelmingly strange to see a good mate in pain and in such a situation.

Aaron is now back home in Northern Ireland and receiving rehab. Together everyone in the Dirty Dozen, as we called our multiple, decided that on October 18 every year we would all get together and catch up.

CHAPTER 16

THE LONG ROAD TO RECOVERY

DOMINIC HAGANS

When I left Selly Oak Hospital on November 2008, I went straight to Headley Court in Surrey for my rehabilitation. It is a fantastic set-up there and I quickly got straight into training. I began by strengthening and conditioning the rest of my body so that when I eventually came out of my wheelchair I would be strong enough to use walking sticks. This was a long battle. I was in my wheelchair for 12 months, and with three weeks' rehab and three weeks' sick leave I felt in my own mind that I was not progressing.

It was good to see my family and get on with life, but I'm a soldier. I used to be able to kick doors down, shoot weapons, and have men at my disposal to train and discipline. Now I look forward to TV and sitting in boredom in my house, pissed off because my mates are out getting pissed up and I'm stuck in a wheelchair trying to get some normality. Over the year I did get out of my wheelchair, but like many other wounded soldiers I still need to have on-going surgery.

On February 6 2009 I was sent back to Selly Oak for a bone graft and to have some muscle moved to my left lower leg. My left tibia and fibula were not growing back to help form the bone, so they had to graft some bone in place. I was in hospital for two days, and then sent home for a week, then back to Headley Court. This only added more setbacks. My backside had been sliced through the buttocks and muscle taken. To get that working again took around a year with constant rehab and physiotherapy, and then once the leg was strong enough I had to learn to walk on my own.

In September 2009 I was put on a scheme to get me back to work part time. I was over the moon to be back in green kit and a soldier again. I worked from 0800 hrs till 1230, and then in the afternoon I could do rehabilitation training in the gym with a physio, which was brilliant. I felt wanted again. But when I started back reality kicked in in the shape of health and safety. While I was still unsteady on my feet I had to have my room converted with grab handles in the shower and around the toilet, and my route to work had to be swept of leaves every day so I didn't fall. It made me feel people were bending over backwards to help me, though this wasn't a problem as we are a family regiment and look after our men.

In February 2010 I had to go back to hospital to have an operation on my left foot. I had bones growing back, but instead of growing into my toes they were growing downwards, so it was like standing on football studs. It was a nightmare in bare feet, especially in the shower.

I kept continuing my rehab, which was brilliant. I went back to work full time, and then in August 2010, after helping the battalion to get ready for a return visit to Afghanistan, I was asked to be the MLO (Military Liaison Officer) at Headley Court. This was a fantastic idea. Who better than an experienced soldier who has himself been injured on operations to do the job? It was easy for me to listen to and understand what men and women like me were going through.

I was looking forward to this fantastic opportunity, but as the battalion had deployed and I was getting ready to move to my new job, my leg became infected and burst open. I was rushed to the new QE Hospital and didn't make my new job. I had to stay in hospital for another six weeks, during which I had seven major operations to remove the infections. My leg was badly infected and the bugs became immune to most antibiotics.

When I left the QE I had to go back to Headley, back in my bloody wheelchair. That was shit – I had gone back six months. They say that sometimes you need a setback to make another step forward. In December 2010 my left leg became red and inflamed again and I was sent by Headley Court for a CT scan which confirmed it was infected again, so I went back to the QE to be put back on antibiotics.

In January 2011 I asked for a second opinion on my leg. Many times I had asked the doctors to remove my leg below the knee, but they declined. I then went to Kings College in London, and after an MRI scan it was apparent that I had osteomyelitis in the bone of my lower left leg, and it was getting worse. I had a long discussion with the surgeon at Kings College, who noticed that my left knee had been damaged in the blast. I have no idea why it had not been spotted before, but thank fuck they never took my leg off below my knee, because in time I would have realised I needed a new knee, and it would not have been strong enough for a below-knee prosthetic. In time I more than likely would have had to have an above-knee amputation, still achievable but at times more complicated?

In April 2011 I had to have another major operation, to remove 6.8 cms of infected bone and clear the infection from my leg. I then had a Taylor Spatial Frame on for a year, which helped to grow a bone while holding it in place – you turn a strut (a sort of big bolt) down a millimetre every day until the bone is complete.

It's June 26 as I write and I have had loads of fluid coming out of my leg today, so my wife frogmarched me to A+E in Birmingham for them to confirm that I had an infection, but they did not understand the frame on my leg. The next day I was taken to Kings College Hospital, where they took one look and admitted me, putting me back on IV antibiotics. It is really doing my head in now.

Well that's where I am today - still no further forward, still having to have more surgery, and yes fed up and pissed off. But more importantly I miss being a soldier. I am more pissed off at having done my job while on operations, yet losing my career.

Do I regret joining the army? Never. If I was 17 I would do it all over again. My biggest regret is having my family put through the ordeal of having the dreaded knock at the door. No soldier would ever want to put his family through that, and for that I'm sorry.

CHAPTER 17

WHERE ARE THEY NOW?

C/SGT JED CUNNINGHAM-EDDAS

After our tour Jed came back and worked as the specialist platoon commander. He was promoted during Op Herrick 13 to Warrant Officer Class 2 and took over from D Coy as the Company Sergeant Major.

SGT ALISTAIR MCKINNEY

Ally has been medically discharged from the army and left the service on the 29th July 2011, completing 22 years' service. He is living with his parents, who care for him daily. His father Frank, also an ex-soldier of the Royal Irish Rangers, commutes from Scotland so he can continue with his work.

SGT BRANGAN

PJ has now been promoted to Warrant Officer Class 2. He returned from Infantry Battle School at Brecon, where he was an instructor, to re-join the Battalion as a CQMS. He has just returned from Afghanistan again, where he was injured in an IED blast, but not seriously, thank god. He has recently taken over as a rifle Company Sergeant Major.

MAJ SIMON SHIRLEY

Major Shirley did get back to work after his rehabilitation for his injury. He became a Company Commander at the Royal Military Academy Sandhurst. He has now completed his army career and left the army in November 2011.

WO2 JOHN CRONIN

WO2 Cronin completed his tour as a Company Sergeant Major, and then took over as the Battalion RQMS for two years before moving to the 1st Battalion Infantry Training Centre at Catterick as the Regimental Sergeant Major. He has completed his tour of duty at Catterick and has now returned to the Battalion as a Commissioned Officer with the rank of Capt. He now has the lucky job of managing soldier's careers within the Battalion and at Training Depots.

RGR ANDY ALLEN

After a long haul of rehabilitation training, Andy moved back to Northern Ireland to be near his family, where he is still in the military. He has raised money on several accounts for other injured soldiers. He also took time out to be monitored at Headley Court for a TV documentary about wounded soldiers.

SGT HUEY BENSON

Huey completed his time as a platoon sergeant and was then promoted to Colour Sergeant, spending a year as a CQMS in a rifle company. He then followed his father's footsteps and moved to the Infantry Battle School in Brecon as an instructor. He has now returned back to the Battalion as a Warrant Officer Class 2, and soon set to take over as D Coy Company Sergeant Major.

CPL PHILLIP GILLESPIE

Phillip has returned to Headley Court several times for rehabilitation training. He is now walking about on his prosthetic leg, though he has been having some problems with bone growing back in his stump and is awaiting further treatment in Birmingham.

CPL TAM DOWIE

Tam completed several military course to further his career, and has not long returned from another tour of Afghanistan.

RGR AARON NIXON

After his injury and spending a long time in the Queen Elizabeth hospital because of his infections, Aaron moved to Headley Court for a week for his rehabilitation. It was decided that he would be better off closer to his family, so he moved back home to Northern Ireland, where he continues with rehabilitation.

RGR PADDY GUY

Paddy is still serving in the regiment and has just completed another tour of Afghanistan.

GLOSSARY

AH - Attack Helicopter - US-designed AH-64 Apaches.

AO - Area of Operations - place where a unit will control and carry out its daily tasks to secure it.

ATO - Ammunition Technical Officer, an extremely professional soldier dedicated to dealing with all types of ammunition and explosive devices.

ARF - Airborne reaction force; troops on standby ready to be moved by air to deal with any situation.

AK47 - Soviet-designed 7.62 mm assault rifle. Over 100 million have been manufactured. Cheap, robust and simple to use.

ANA - Afghan National Army.

ANP - Afghan National Police.

CASEVAC - Casualty Evacuation of personnel from the battlefield.

Camp Bastion - The main military base in Helmand Province, Afghanistan.

Camp Shorabak - The main military base for the Afghan National Army in Helmand Province, located next to Camp Bastion.

CQMS - Company Quartermaster Sergeant.

C/SGT - Colour Sergeant.

CPL - Corporal.

CGC - Conspicuous Gallantry Cross. Medal issued for bravery.

CSM - Company Sergeant Major, a warrant officer.

Chinook - A large helicopter designed for moving troops and equipment around.

DC - District Centre.

EN - The enemy.

ECM - Electronic Counter Measures. Equipment designed to help combat remote-controlled IEDS - (Improvised Explosive Devices).

FOB - Forward Operating Base. An area where troops have occupied in order to launch operations from.

FFD - First Field Dressing. A medical dressing applied as soon as possible after attending to a casualty.

FIBUA - Fighting in Built up Areas. Military operations conducted in buildings.

FLET - Forward Line of Enemy Troops - the boundary line where the enemy is occupying land.

GPMG - General Purpose Machine Gun. A 7.62 mm caliber machine gun that can be used on a bipod, tripod or mounted on a vehicle or in an aircraft. Rate of fire 750 rounds per minute.

HE - High Explosive.

IED - Improvised Explosive Device.

IRT - Incident Response Team, the group of medics and soldiers on 24 hour-a-day standby at Camp Bastion to carry out medical evacuations across Helmand Province. From 2008 referred to as MERT (Medical Emergency Response Team).

ISAF - International Security and Assistance Force. The name given for military intervention in to Afghanistan. It was created in December 2001 after the Taliban were ousted from power by Operation Enduring Freedom.

KANDAK - A battalion of soldiers in the Afghan National Army.

L/CPL - Lance Corporal.

LT - Lieutenant.

MIST - A report given over the radio to update the medical team on casualties - Mechanism of injury (how it happened), Injury, vital Signs (an update on any signs getting worse) and Treatment.

MERT - Medical Emergency Response Team. A team of dedicated soldiers and medics on standby to extract casualties from the battlefield.

MFC - Mortar Fire Controller. A professional soldier who can bring heavy mortar fire down on the enemy.

OMLT - Operational Mentoring Liaison Team. This is made up of British troops who help to train the Afghan Army and support them on missions.

PINZ - A military vehicle built with limited armour, used to transport soldiers and small equipment.

PKM - Pulemyot Kalashnikov Modernizirovannyi, better known as the Kalashnikov machine gun. Designed by Mikhail Kalashnikov in the early 1960s, it was put into service with the Soviet Armed Forces and is currently in production in Russia. It fires a 7.62 x 54mm round at a rate of around 750 rounds per minute and has an effective range of 1500 meters.

PRR - Personal Role Radio.

RSOI - Reception Staging and Onward Integration. Further training before soldiers can deploy on the ground.

RGR - Ranger - a rank in the Royal Irish (the equivalent of private in other regiments).

SA80 - The British Army standard individual rifle, 5.56 mm caliber.

SANGAR - A fortified defence position built by soldiers to help protect them from enemy fire while on sentry duty.

TacSat - Tactical Satellite communications equipment.

WARRIOR - An armoured personnel carrier, designed to move troops around the battlefield and give supporting fire.

WIMIK - A Land Rover fitted with a Weapons Mount Installation Kit which allows it to become a platform for a variety of weapons.